CCCC STUDIES IN WRITING & RHETORIC
Edited by Victor Villanueva, Washington State Unit

I0128835

The aim of the CCCC Studies in Writing & Rhetoric Series is to influence how we think about language in action and especially how writing gets taught at the college level. The methods of studies vary from the critical to historical to linguistic to ethnographic, and their authors draw on work in various fields that inform composition—including rhetoric, communication, education, discourse analysis, psychology, cultural studies, and literature. Their focuses are similarly diverse—ranging from individual writers and teachers, to work on classrooms and communities and curricula, to analyses of the social, political, and material contexts of writing and its teaching.

SWR was one of the first scholarly book series to focus on the teaching of writing. It was established in 1980 by the Conference on College Composition and Communication (CCCC) in order to promote research in the emerging field of writing studies. As our field has grown, the research sponsored by SWR has continued to articulate the commitment of CCCC to supporting the work of writing teachers as reflective practitioners and intellectuals.

We are eager to identify influential work in writing and rhetoric as it emerges. We thus ask authors to send us project proposals that clearly situate their work in the field and show how they aim to redirect our ongoing conversations about writing and its teaching. Proposals should include an overview of the project, a brief annotated table of contents, and a sample chapter. They should not exceed 10,000 words.

To submit a proposal, please register as an author at www.editorial manager.com/nctebp. Once registered, follow the steps to submit a proposal (be sure to choose SWR Book Proposal from the drop-down list of article submission types).

FROM BOYS TO MEN

RHETORICS OF EMERGENT AMERICAN MASCULINITY

Leigh Ann Jones

Hunter College of the City University of New York

Conference on College Composition and Communication

National Council of Teachers of English

NCTE

Staff Editor: Bonny Graham
Series Editor: Victor Villanueva
Interior Design: Mary Rohrer
Cover Design: Mary Rohrer and Lynn Weckhorst

NCTE Stock Number: 03753; eStock Number: 03760
ISBN 978-0-8141-0375-3; eISBN 978-0-8141-0376-0

It is the policy of NCTE in its journals and other publications to provide a forum for the open discussion of ideas concerning the content and the teaching of English and the language arts. Publicity accorded to any particular point of view does not imply endorsement by the Executive Committee, the Board of Directors, or the membership at large, except in announcements of policy, where such endorsement is clearly specified.

Every effort has been made to provide current URLs and email addresses, but because of the rapidly changing nature of the Web, some sites and addresses may no longer be accessible.

Publication partially funded by a subvention grant from the Conference on College Composition and Communication of the National Council of Teachers of English.

Library of Congress Cataloging-in-Publication Data

Names: Jones, Leigh Ann, author.
Title: From boys to men : rhetorics of emergent American masculinity / Leigh
   Ann Jones.
Description: Urbana, IL : Conference on College Composition and Communi-
   cation of the National Council of Teachers of English, [2016] | Series: Studies
   in writing and rhetoric | Includes bibliographical references and index.
Identifiers: LCCN 2016006871 (print) | LCCN 2016020955 (ebook) | ISBN
   9780814103753 ((pbk) : alk. paper) | ISBN 9780814103760 ()
Subjects: LCSH: Masculinity—Study and teaching—United States. | Young
   men—Study and teaching—United States. | Men—United States—Identity.
   | Nationalism—United States. | Youth—United States—Societies and clubs.
   | Rhetoric—United States.
Classification: LCC HQ1090.3 .J664 2016 (print) | LCC HQ1090.3 (ebook) |
   DDC 155.3/32—dc23
LC record available at https://lccn.loc.gov/2016006871

for Olivier
and for my parents

CONTENTS

ACKNOWLEDGMENTS

I AM DEEPLY GRATEFUL FOR THE MANY people who gave me information, advice, feedback, support, encouragement, and friendship during the years I wrote this book. SWR Series Editor Victor Villanueva saw the potential in an early manuscript and encouraged me to build it into the study that appears here, offering wise suggestions. He has long been a source of advice, for which I am sincerely thankful. I thank Bonny Graham at NCTE for her insightful editing that helped fine-tune the book during the production process. I also thank Krista Ratcliffe, whose review of an early version of my manuscript was especially constructive during my revising process, as were the comments of an anonymous reviewer. The idea for this book originally took form as my dissertation at the University of Arizona, and I thank Ken McAllister, who advised me on that project, and Roxanne Mountford, who advised me then and well beyond that phase of my work.

At Hunter College, I am lucky to have wonderfully encouraging and warm colleagues. I cannot offer enough thanks to Cristina Alfar, whose support of my work during her years as chair of the English department has been immeasurable and invaluable. I'm also thankful for the department's current chair, Sarah Chinn, for her support of my work and for her collegial optimism. I particularly appreciate the support of English colleagues and friends Trudy Smoke, Sonali Perera, Amy Robbins, Barbara Webb, Angela Reyes, and Wendy Hayden, who have helped me feel at home in the academy, as well as Candice Jenkins, now at the University of Illinois at Urbana–Champaign, who suggested helpful sources at an early stage of my work on the manuscript. I am also grateful to anthropology colleague and friend Michael Steiper, ever encouraging and funny. And I thank my undergraduate and graduate students, who

ix

I love working with; they regularly teach me as much about rhetoric as I teach them.

Beyond Hunter, CUNY has a robust community of rhetoric and composition scholars across New York City that I am thankful to be a part of. Particular gratitude goes to Timothy McCormack and Mark McBeth at John Jay College, Corey Mead at Baruch College, and Amy Wan at Queens College. I also thank Maria Jerskey, my good friend and colleague at LaGuardia Community College, whose warmth, optimism, and excellent cooking have meant a great deal to me and whose suggestions on the pedagogy chapter of this book were crucial.

My institution has provided me with generous support for this project in the form of two PSC-CUNY grants and a CUNY Faculty Fellowship Publication Program award. My advisor for the latter, Lynn Chancer, was particularly encouraging and generous with her time. My cohort in that program provided useful feedback; in particular, Lucia Trimbur's insightful responses to my drafts and her friendship were significant to my writing process. Additionally, the staff at the Columbia University Archives and Columbiana Library was graciously helpful while I was researching there.

For their support in the form of a successful writing group, I thank friends and fellow writers Kimberly Helmer from the University of California, Santa Cruz, and Emily Bauman from New York University, who read and commented generously on early drafts of manuscript chapters, also providing laughter and lunch companionship.

Support and reality checks from friends have sustained me throughout this project. For that, I thank my dear friends Arianne Burford and Angela Mullis, academics both, who have provided a much-needed refuge from work life. Alexander Baxter offered a generous ear when I needed it. Mark Treshock's support in the form of a quiet place to write, along with his consistent common sense and encouragement, was essential to my work. Gene Jerskey's inquisitive energy and refined conversation skills along the way have been a delightful reminder that writing can be enjoyable.

Finally, I thank Olivier, who presented his intelligence and open heart to me at exactly the right moment and who is helping me imagine the possible. And thank you to my parents, Denney and Linda Clements Jones, for teaching me to appreciate an origin story in whatever form it may present itself, and my sister, Kimberly Jones Routt, for her sense of humor about the stories in which we've found ourselves.

1

Coming of Age as a Boy in America: Emerging Masculinity as Rhetoric

A COLUMN TITLED "FROM BOYS TO MEN" IN the *New York Times* on October 15, 2010, proclaimed the arrival of "A New Masculine Ideal" in male runway models. But rather than a new ideal, the article describes the return on that year's catwalks and magazine pages from the image of a "juvenile with pipe-cleaner proportions" that prevailed during the previous decade to a more "conventional" image of men. The author cites the troublesome economy as a call for this return:

> You lose the T-shirt and the skateboard. You buy an interview suit and a package of Gillette Mach 3 blades. You grow up, in other words. Suddenly evidence of a new phase in the cycle of evolving masculine imagery was all over the catwalks in the runway season that recently ended. Just as suddenly it can be seen splashed across the covers of magazines, where the boys of recent memory have been transformed overnight into men. (Trebay)

According to Trebay, this posttransformation image of manhood reflects American men's desire to imagine themselves as workers during a time of soaring unemployment in the United States. But the image itself and Trebay's interpretation of it rely on a deeper cultural narrative in which the transformation from boyhood to masculinity—"growing up," as Trebay calls it—is a key focus. What is involved in this transformation? Trebay's column suggests that the change means choosing different images to represent manhood, but in fact the images themselves rely on a broader sense of American masculine identity. In that broader narrative that frames identity, the male models and, by extension, American males in general are actors whose actions mimic the transformations of American adolescent males generally. The actors are alternately "boys" and "men" depending on their body types and where they fall within the narrative chronology, and within Trebay's language they are also "you" in both cases. The actions include "los[ing] the T-shirt and skateboard" and "buy[ing] an interview suit and a package of Gillette Mach 3 blades." A rhetorical reading of the article reveals that the men on the runway transform in response to the current economy, changing not just their behavior but also the nature of their maleness. The article's narrative presents masculinity as emerging through a process of choices and behaviors that, if successful, result in true American maleness.

The Trebay article both mystifies and reifies a process of moving from boy to man, a masculine transformation, and it is worth analyzing because it is representative; the rhetorical creation of this transformation process from a pre-masculine to a masculine state is perhaps the most fundamental element of representations of masculinity in the United States. Similar to many identity-marking efforts, Trebay's article defines masculinity against what it is not, and it is these concrete definitions that create the background for the transformation story: a real man is not a boy because a man shaves, is large-framed, wears a suit; a boy is not a man because a boy can't shave, is small, doesn't wear a suit because he isn't active in the economy. Mystified by the article but yet essential to it is the idea of transformation that links these two sides of the binary with its implied argument that it is possible to become a man, but not guaranteed. The process portrayed indirectly through the images and accompanying narrative is highly consequential: becoming a man in this context can be as easy as purchasing the right implements, but failing to do so means failing economically and as a representative male person.

Yet this transformation process involves more than buying or wearing something; it requires a change in discourse that manifests through rhetorical moves. In *A Rhetoric of Motives*, Kenneth Burke provides insight into why the process is so deep-reaching in its power to shape behavior:

> [A]n adolescent, eager to "grow up," is trained by our motion pictures to meditate much on the imagery of brutality and murder, as the most noteworthy signs of action in an ideal or imaginary adult world. By the time he is fifteen, he has "witnessed" more violence than most soldiers or gunmen experience in a lifetime. And he has "participated in" all this imagery, "empathically reënacting" it. Thus initiated, he might well think of "growing up" (that is, of "transformation") in such excessive terms. His awareness of himself as a developing person requires a vocabulary. (17–18)

These two views of masculinity that Trebay and Burke call attention to, one of money-earning, suit-wearing self-control and the other of conditioned acceptance of violence, demonstrate two different and potentially contradictory images of masculinity that result from the process of "transformation." While the authors of these two different images construct our ideas of what is possible for males, Burke suggests with his quotation marks that the process of masculine "transformation" is itself a concept that boys are primed to accept from birth. Thus, the transformation is rhetorically constructed and demands a change in rhetorical action.

I argue that Burke offers the most useful analytical framework for understanding this rhetorical process of masculine transformation—a use to which Burke's writings have not yet been put, but which can accommodate the contradictions and various results that have emerged from masculine transformation rhetoric, such as the two versions of masculinity described here. While gender theorists have provided much guidance in understanding the social construction of masculinity and its intersections with race, class, sexuality, and ability, a rhetorical approach is needed to demonstrate how language works socially to induce popular participation in the process of its construction.

I engage here with the masculine transformation process as it has been institutionalized in organizations in the United States, even though the process is not limited to such sites. American boys attain the vocabulary Burke points to from sites as disparate as the self-consciously performative space of the fashion runway, the easy entertainment of films and television, and the remote authority of the geneticists' laboratory, all of which make claims about masculinity's vitality and fundamental function in American lives. These claims form narratives about mainstream manhood that sometimes swirl around us obliquely, including stories of cultivating manhood over time and others of more contracted crucible experiences. Our interpretations of physical manhood and the journey boys take into its space underwrite popular culture and social experience, forming a significant element of the way many people in the United States understand themselves. Institutional, organized expressions of male coming-of-age rhetoric, the concern of this monograph, encourage American audiences to believe that emergent masculinity is an enduring natural phenomenon and an essential component of American identity, and that the outcomes of the transformation process have important consequences for the United States as a nation.

Because this idea of transformation is socially produced and performed in public spaces that intersect with institutional spaces, organizations for boys provide the best specific places to find examples of its workings. Looking throughout the twentieth century in the United States, one finds narratives of male development in many organizations for boys, sites that have received broad social, familial, and state support. The groups that I analyze here have been able to gain strong cultural support because their language and practices have become such an intrinsic part of American identity that we are guided to believe that membership is part of proper male citizenship grooming. These organizations have presented this citizenship grooming as the road boys must follow in order to cultivate good character. In each case, American ideas about boyhood have resulted not from direct public appeals to credibility, emotion, or data, but rather through rhetorical genres, including ritualized statements and symbols such as the US Army's "Soldier's Creed" and the Boy Scouts of America's origin myth. Through these genres, the organizations have tapped into young males' consciousness, shaping their identities and invoking them as incipient members of the nation. Organizations for boys are an excellent example of the role of Burkean identification in crafting the tie between consciousness of the nation as a "community" and popular conceptions of the developing boy during the last century. Yet they also point to significant ambiguity as they push boys to identify with the overarching imagined community of Americans through the fog of class antagonism, as citizens who would resolve the problem of individualism that remains in tension with national unity, and as warriors who would symbolically forward national, imperial expansion despite the controversial accompanying violence.

The process of imagining a movement from boyhood to manhood is a rhetorical undertaking not just because of its effect on individual American boys, but also because it requires large groups of people to identify with a particular conception of destiny or teleology and in so identifying, to conceive of boys as agents in a broader scene that expands to national boundaries. The mental and physical discipline applied to boys through youth organizations stems from ideologically driven theories of male and childhood development, and these theories have been applied rhetorically through origin stories, credos, public statements, and other symbols. American youth organizations have been one powerful node from which complex rhetorics of national manhood have emanated. The rhetorical process of transforming ideology into practice invokes—*interpellates*, to use Louis Althusser's term—boys' consciousness of who they are by addressing them and then limiting the possibilities for their identification (173). Race, class, sexuality, and ability attend the identification process for boys and create dialectics between hegemonic masculinity and a myriad of marginalized identities.

My primary concern here is with the role of this potential ambiguity in hegemonic young male identification, and in a particular pattern of using the idea of "transformation" as an attempt to reconcile the ambiguities that arise in the process of constituting male identity. I join other rhetoricians who have engaged masculinity theories and whose work has pointed to the need to understand more thoroughly how communication functions in and through masculinity as a discourse that arranges cultural practices and that brings about material consequences. Early rhetorical work on masculinity effectively made the case for addressing masculinity in the field of composition and rhetoric, though that work remains incomplete. Specifically, Robert Connors pointed out that "throughout most of Western History . . . [t]he historical discipline of rhetoric was shaped by male rituals, male contests, male ideals, and masculine agendas" (139), drawing on Walter Ong's history of agonistic ritual and men's insecurity-driven struggles for control (140). Connors notes that in the absence of effective male role models, boys have resorted to organizations like the YMCA that impose social controls and rituals bestowing manhood upon them, but that today fraternities provide the only option for this type of guidance. While critical of these organizational sites of manhood, Connors continues to search for a source of identity transformation that will account for boys' emotional needs—a replacement for initiation rites that can resolve the alienation that he argues many men feel as they fail to reconcile the social roles they are expected to fulfill with the emotions they are unable to make sense of.

To some extent, then, Connors sees masculinity rhetoric as a response to manhood-in-crisis. Deepening a dialogue on masculinity rhetoric, Luke Winslow questions the predominant popular narrative of masculinity-in-crisis that often reifies a conception of gender as biologically fixed, emerging from a single homogenous foundation. In his dissertation, "Style and Struggle: The Rhetoric of Masculinity," he instead proposes that masculinity is act-oriented rather than agent-oriented or fixed in the nature of the person, paraphrasing Burke: "Like women, men need to define themselves—they can't just *be*" (27). Winslow makes central the performance inherent in masculinity.

James V. Catano's study *Ragged Dicks: Masculinity, Steel, and the Rhetoric of the Self-Made Man* takes a psychoanalytic approach to the rhetoric of masculinity, arguing in line with Judith Butler (140) that masculinity is "rule-governed[,] . . . performed and maintained—culturally and individually—through and in terms of preset rhetorical arguments" (Catano 2). He asserts that the myth of the self-made man covers its rhetorical tracks by obfuscating the contradiction between the myth and the relative class immobility and income disparity in the United States. This contradiction also surrounds the myths of the male youth organizations that I analyze here, making clear that the sources of such "preset rhetorical arguments" are worth uncovering and scrutinizing with the rhetorical tools available.

Perhaps closest to the theoretical spirit of my inquiry but furthest from its historical location, Lindsay Green McManus uses Erving Goffman's work on performativity to understand what she calls the "true, psychological self" that manifests through performances of masculinity. In her dissertation, "Performing Masculinity: Control, Manhood, and the Rhetoric of Effeminacy," she analyzes masculinity in Quintilian's rhetorical work and in literature from the Renaissance to the nineteenth century, asserting that in each case masculinity was defined through its opposition to effeminacy. This binary between masculinity and femininity that is inherent in masculine performances is also key to the identity-forming activities of youth organizations for boys in the United States, and McManus is correct in locating rhetoric within gender performance. I depart from her argument when she groups manhood performance with masculinity performance, however. As I outline in the following paragraphs, masculinity in the United States is an outgrowth of a particular historical relationship to economics and race that manifested within American gender performances at the end of the nineteenth and beginning of the twentieth centuries.

Outside of rhetorical scholarship, in the broader world, contemporary public assertions about how boys develop into men are situated within conversations about the US nation, race, class, labor, medicine, and education at various points in the last century. The result of these overlapping discourses is what we receive today as a mainstream idea—that there is an American man, characterized by his role in daily life and in exceptional circumstances—and a preoccupation among parents, educators, doctors, and community leaders with how members of a national "community" can build that American man from a boy. The American man is discursively positioned as a metonym for the American in particular historical moments. While coded as hegemonic masculinity, the performance of manhood at these moments is at the same time presented as a universal performance of Americanness. The cultural preoccupation with building that Americanness, and building the American boy into a man who embodies it, is funneled most coherently through organizations outside of formal schooling, though these organizations act in tandem with formal, particularly public, schooling. The distinction between formal education and the training by extracurricular organizations is relevant because it explains why youth organizations have persisted for boys from a wide range of political, class, and religious backgrounds.

To help explain the role of formal education as opposed to extracurricular training, Ian Hunter's work examines the nearly universally shared ideal of principled education through school systems, an ideal that relies on the belief in the liberal subject and the importance of that subject's development. Hunter argues that in reality, rather than a deliberate, systematic means of fostering such principled development, schooling is primarily an "improvised assemblage as a device to meet the contingencies of a particular history" (xvii)—a device that historically has reflected the most advanced bureaucratic technologies available for schooling at a particular time rather than any fundamental idealistic principles. These bureaucratic technologies have effectively separated the development of students' civic identities from the development of their spiritual consciousness, making the civic the realm of government institutions and leaving the spiritual and moral development to other social forces (xxii–xxiii).

This separation that Hunter describes has created a perceived need for nongovernmental institutions such as the Boy Scouts of America (BSA) and college fraternities to take up the task of spiritual and moral development for youth. The function of the US Army is more ambiguous than that of the BSA and fraternities, as the army is clearly a government institution but has adopted language of spiritual and moral development in its recruiting campaigns and its creeds. The chapters that follow address the bridge between civic development and spiritual/moral development that the three organizations form, attending to the tensions and contradictions that arise between the two goals. I examine these contradictions by applying Burke's lens of rhetoric as identity performance from *A Rhetoric of Motives*, focusing on the organizations' semipublic and public textual performances.

In the following section, I describe a theory of identification that I later use to explore the ways these performances function rhetorically, and then I briefly summarize how nationalism and masculinity function as intertwined components of males' identification as emergent, masculine American subjects.

UNDERSTANDING IDENTITY-BUILDING RHETORIC IN ORGANIZATIONS FOR BOYS

While national masculinity has been constructed in and for public spaces, it has also been formulated in more quotidian language acts in the private space of the family and semiprivate meeting spaces of community organizations. Rather than functioning as explicitly public appeals, masculinity and nationalism are best understood as effects arising when audiences identify with the discourse that is presented in these semipublic spaces. These effects are then carried home into the most private spaces, as well as publicized in the most public spaces. Figures such as community authorities create nationalism and masculinity in this way by invoking audiences as part of a natural, predetermined, and enduring community, and audiences, so interpellated, carry their identities as a framework for understanding and performing themselves publicly and privately.

A rhetorical analysis of the rhetoric of emergent masculinity must explain how language functions in this interpellation to convince young males to imagine themselves as masculine in response to the complex situations they encounter. Gender theorist R. W. Connell writes that "practice . . . always responds to a situation, and situations are structured in ways that admit certain possibilities and not others" (65). And as language practices, the possibilities for rhetorics of manhood are worked out in such constrained situations. Aristotle explained rhetorical responses to such constraints through the concepts of *kairos* (opportunity) and *to prepon* (appropriateness). In the same tradition, Lloyd Bitzer argued that rhetorical responses are attuned to particular exigencies (9–13). For the most part, rhetoric scholars understand that discourse is created from a mass of such specific settings, for particular audiences, and by speakers or writers who present particular versions of their characters. Yet as Richard Vatz has argued seminally, we should not be limited by Bitzer's classical understanding of rhetoric as persuasion, which relies on the notion of a fixed, preexisting speaker, audience, and context for argument. Bitzer's model fails to account for the complexity involved in gender identity that Connell describes. As gender theorists have made clear, gender is a construction, and the notion of a fixed, preexisting audience does not adequately explain how gender is constructed through language.

Much more useful is Burke's notion of rhetoric as performance wherein subjectivity and identity, as well as a rhetorical situation, are created within a situation rather than assumed (*Rhetoric*). This model allows for the constraints on subjectivity that come from outside an individual, but also allows for a range of possible responses that in turn create the situation itself.

Burke's dramatistic paradigm explains how language moves boys and young men to imagine themselves as masculine Americans in this way, creating a rhetorical situation and a performance of the self. By pulling rhetoric away from a classical understanding of public discourse as appeals to *ethos*, *pathos*, and *logos*—character, emotion, and logic—and placing it into a world of actions and words executed in the drama of everyday life, he describes rhetorical situations in the modern world as "modes of action" that involve a scene (setting or situation), act (thing done), agent (actor), agency (method of doing), and purpose (*Grammar* xxii). These elements make up a rhetorical situation in which a person imagines himself to fit in a particular way. Applying these terms to particular cases, Burke finds that ratios between two of them typically serve as a "container" and a "thing contained" (3). That is, one element— usually the scene or the act—forms the background and justification for the other—typically the act, agent, agency, or purpose, though other ratios are possible. Burke's ratios allow rhetoricians to explain rhetorical situations in terms of consistencies, inconsistencies, and complexities between a backdrop and a foreground, a kind of reworking of the premise and the conclusion.

Burke's essential contribution to rhetoric is his argument that humans are persuaded to act by identifying with other humans, and in making this argument, he redefines rhetoric as identification rather than persuasion. Through the drama of rhetorical situations, people imagine themselves to be "consubstantial"—that is, they identify—with others. He points out that "[a] doctrine of *consubstantiality*, either explicit or implicit, may be necessary to any way of life. . . . [A]nd a way of life is an *acting-together*; and in acting together, men have common sensations, concepts, images, ideas, attitudes that make them *consubstantial* (*Rhetoric* 21). Burke understood that the banal actions that make up our "way of life" are motivated by a deep need to belong, but also that the terms of that belonging precede us. Often, the process of identifying with these terms is unplanned and unconscious (*Language* 301).

Because the chapters that follow are ultimately an ideological critique of cultural practices, I want to clarify what I mean by appeals and why appeals are inherently ideological in the context of my Burkean reading of masculinity rhetoric, and so need to turn to the history that explains the way rhetoricians have understood the relationship between rhetors and audiences, beginning with the constitutive model of rhetoric. The constitutive model is important not just as a way to understand this exchange of linguistic effects on audiences, but also as a particular way to conceive of the meaning and function of appeals themselves in rhetoric. When I locate and analyze appeals in male youth organizations, I understand those appeals as events that develop and reify the participants' subjectivity, as well as the rhetorical situations themselves. In this conception, rhetorical appeals are performance. An understanding of the rhetorical process as performance has evolved during the twentieth century to position appeals as ideological and ethical rather than merely mechanical effects because, in the constitutive model, they are an act of world disclosure, a way of publicly imagining the world and the self within that world. In contrast, the classical (influence) model positions rhetoric as a goal-oriented activity, the implications of which hinge on the question of whether the rhetor is successful or has failed within a world that is established and unchangeable, as Ronald Walter Greene has pointed out.

For Aristotle, the touchstone source of classically based modern understandings of rhetoric, appeals were measured as persuasive effects on audiences: he described rhetoric famously in Book II of *On Rhetoric* as "the faculty of observing in any given case the available means of persuasion." Aristotle saw these available means as observable to the skilled rhetorician because they respond to a preexisting relationship of influence between speaker and audience. Aristotle explicated his types of appeals and connected them to the variety of possible audience dispositions that may pose as variables in a rhetorical situation. So reliable and fixed were these means of persuasion and this model of influence for Aristotle and his progeny that Renaissance rhetoricians suggested pupils practice an abundance of possible arguments beforehand and choose from among those in their mental toolbox when they needed to persuade an audience. Rhetoricians in the Aristotelian tradition generally held that such a catalog of appeals, executed selectively by a practiced rhetor, would lead to the persuasive effect that the rhetor desired. In this context, an appeal was a strategy that influenced an audience by changing their minds or their actions, and the appeal's success was based on whether it achieved that effect. No attention was paid to how audiences rethought the world or reimagined themselves as a result of the appeal.

This classically based understanding of rhetoric as persuasion permeates our contemporary theory and analysis. Greene refers to this conceptualization as the "influence model of effectivity." But to say that public argument or public artifacts are rhetorical because they are persuasive misses a key development in the field of rhetoric, which is the understanding of rhetoric as performance rather than straightforward persuasion, a development that began with Burke and evolved through the second half of the twentieth century into the constitutive model discussed earlier in this chapter. As Greene points out, "a constitutive model of rhetorical effectivity privileges identification over persuasion as the key to unpacking the rhetorical nature of public argument." This model is elided, Greene argues, in the "constant repetition that rhetoric is a form of persuasion." To correct this elision, we need to apply to public argument the constitutive model with its conception of rhetoric as identification, understanding that identification implicates audiences beyond their immediate responses to a predefined rhetorical situation. And because rhetoric as identification enables and transforms the subject, it has a much deeper cultural reach than a persuasion model of rhetoric suggests. In inventing a worldview and a truth, rhetorical appeals are ideological. To borrow from Edwin Black's argument in "The Second Persona" as historicized by Greene, rhetoric invokes a particular type of audience and in so doing invokes an ideology, "ideology in the sense that Marx used the term: the network of interconnected convictions that functions in a man [or woman] epistemically and that shapes his [or her] identity by determining how he [or she] views the world" (qtd. in Greene).[1]

Because identification is ideological, seemingly minor or private (but repeated) instances of rhetoric that lead to national identification are crucial sites for rhetoricians, as these rhetorical moments form concepts of self and a relationship to what we think of as a "community," justifying significant actions by invoking commonplace values and concepts. We often find these commonplaces coded in key words and phrases such as *character* that are repeated in a variety of media and institutions from a broad political spectrum, and they also play out in our intimate relationships with friends and family. None of us is free from the ideological working of nationalist rhetoric. The rhetorician's job is to locate the ideologies that undergird the appeals they help form, working backwards to identify the values and subject-forming processes behind them. Rhetorical criticism becomes a "hermeneutic reading strategy dedicated to interpreting the meaning of the text based on how it positions an audience" (Greene). Drawing from Barbara Beisecker's 1989 article "Rethinking the Rhetorical Situation from within the Thematic of *Différance*," I find that for rhetoricians a central ethical question is, how does a text make possible a subjectivity?

In engaging an ideological, performance-based critique of rhetoric, Burke helps rhetors follow the connection between ideology and language acts by describing four terms or "tropes." These tropes, from "Four Master Tropes" in the appendix to *A Grammar of Motives,* provide a useful vocabulary for discussing language acts as appeals and provide further nuance to his pentad framework. For Burke they are the four structures through which we experience "the truth" (503). As such, we could say that they reveal the structures through which a worldview is created. These tropes include metaphor, metonymy, synecdoche, and irony, and when they explain not literature but our experience of reality, Burke translates them as perspective, reduction, representation, and dialectic, respectively. Perspective (metaphor) tells us how a character is unique, different from other characters. So a boy participating in an organization might, for example, be seen through the perspective of his physical being or moral character, two perspectives that the Boy Scouts of America has taken. These perspectives are a way to explain human motivation (504).

In using reduction (metonymy), we use terms of the tangible to speak of the intangible, Burke explains (*Grammar* 506). For example, in the US military's "Army of One" recruiting campaign, images of physical attributes—soldiers in uniform, standing erect, with bodies of roughly the same height—stand in for intangible characteristics such as self-control. And as Burke notes, "a reduction is a representation" (507). All of the tropes overlap for Burke, and in the analyses that follow, we see how perspective—for example, that of a boy—overlaps with reduction, such as that of a boy in uniform standing at attention, and those categories overlap with representation, such as that of a boy in uniform standing as a representative of the nation's future.

Burke explains that synecdoche is at work in any political theory of representation: "[I]n a complex civilization," he writes, "any act of representation automatically implies a synecdochic relationship (insofar as the act is, or is held to be, 'truly representative')" (*Grammar* 508). The rhetoric of youth organizations discussed in this study calls out boys as representative of the nation or particular national agendas.

When different agents act together, they participate in the rhetorical dialectic of Burke's formulation. In their individual perspectives, agents may reveal themselves to have different motivations from others; however, they act with others in spite of the difference, and for Burke this collective action as dialectic is the social equivalent of the literary trope of irony. The trope of dialectic explains how in the case of organizations for boys, their character-building activities exist alongside temptations; attention to family structure exists alongside urban development and a perceived dissolution of structure and values that accompanies it; the promise of the marketplace exists alongside the dying dream of individual wealth; and national progress exists alongside national violence and perceived weakness. The agents in conversations about boys include progressives and imperialists, advocates for nonviolence and militarists, feminists and advocates of conventional gender norms, and educators and defense spenders. These seemingly contradictory positions within the same organization arise from ambiguities in an organization's terms of identification, a condition I elaborate on a bit later.

Other scholars have extended Burke's model to account more fully for the effects of identification on large groups of people who imagine themselves to have a common purpose and common inborn characteristics, such as those who consider themselves to be a version of ideal American men. Rhetorician Maurice Charland theorizes that such identification is rhetorical, arguing that rather than members constituting a nation, in fact nationalist language constitutes members through rhetoric that invokes them as a "people" through a series of "narrative ideological effects" (134). He examines this process in proclamations made by Quebec's movement for political sovereignty. Building on this idea that political subjectivity is built through a process of identification, I argue that the process of constituting membership through rhetorical identification takes place not just during grand historical or political moments such as the drafting of a constitution; it often happens over the course of more banal moments that are repeated in the form of private and public rituals and habits. Through these rituals and habits, citizens learn of themselves as national subjects by reading documents in institutions such as schools and churches and by voluntary membership in organizations that provide language that grooms individuals in particular directions from an early age. Michael Billig refers to the national ideology that emerges from such daily discourse as "banal nationalism." For Billig the "beliefs, assumptions, habits, representations and practices" that are reproduced in mundane, everyday actions are the most persuasive elements of nationalism, more persuasive than singular rhetorical responses to national events (6). He argues that "the metonymic image of banal nationalism is not a flag which is being consciously waved with fervent passion; it is the flag hanging unnoticed on the public building" (8). While organizations for boys have engaged in conscious and passionate flag waving in public presentations, their more common rituals have become mundane elements of American childhood and family life that have created national subjectivity for boys for at least a century and a half.

My analysis is an attempt to break down the processes by which some of those organizations for boys have enacted identification through the language of rituals, statements, and creeds, rhetorical moves that together form both exceptional and banal instances of masculine national identification. In this process, we see examples of how identification is troubled by economy, gender, race, and sexuality.

When we understand the way in which some of these organizations for boys have operated rhetorically throughout the history of masculinity in the United States, we can better understand how we arrive at our rhetorical practices today and why they are of concern to academic rhetoricians. For example, we can see how a book like 2012 Republican presidential hopeful Rick Perry's *On My Honor: Why the American Values of the Boy Scouts Are Worth Fighting For* is not just a story of a shaping influence in the political candidate's life, but an opening for his assertion of his character as affirmation of his Americanness, and that it sends a clear message that Perry identifies—and offers an identity for other males—as a hegemonic, unambiguously masculine male in the face of a confusing economic and political climate.

And those of us who teach rhetoric and composition can use this history to inform our classroom practices. Because rhetorics of emergent masculinity invoke all of the students we teach, both male and female, it is a particularly rich subject for study. It also creates a particularly useful site of analysis through which students can begin to understand the role of rhetoric in forming subjectivity and identity. To push the possibilities further, the rhetorics of emergent masculinity can be an inroad to an inquiry into civic engagement in the United States. If students understand how they are constructed through narratives at the nexus of gender, race, class, and sexuality, they can begin to question assumed identities and reconceive their own agency within US democracy.

NATIONALISM AND RHETORIC

As masculinity is configured through language in the United States, it is typically tied to a sense of belonging to an American national community. Nationalism is a structured practice that, in concert with masculinity, "admits certain possibilities and limits others," to once again refer to Connell's phrase, and therefore is an important constraint for rhetoricians to attend to in considering how masculinities proliferate through language in American organizations for boys. In recent years, rhetoricians have begun to reexamine the ways that nationalism manifests as possibilities and limitations. Commenting on Burke's description of the nation as a scene that creates identity among citizens, Gregory Clark notes that it "explains the covert as well as overt rhetorical ways in which individuals are prompted to recreate themselves in the image of a collective identity" (4). Burke himself saw the United States as a community put into practice by people who identify as citizens and then abide by the constraints on the possibilities for action among its members. Searching for markers of their personal meaning and value, Burke explained, citizens find scenes that "place a person in his own eyes, as he surrounds himself with a scene which, he is assured, attests to his moral quality. For he can feel that he participates in the quality that the scene itself is thought to possess" (qtd. in Clark 3).

Examining the nation as a rhetorically constructed space helps us to understand the idea of a nation as an "imagined political community," as Benedict Anderson has influentially defined it (6). Anderson, whose definition has been a starting point for many subsequent studies of nationalism, describes a nation as a community that we imagine as "both inherently limited and sovereign" (5–6). His definition contributes to a larger conversation about nationalism that attributes the phenomenon to causes ranging from an intangible sense of common spirit, as Renan argued in 1882, to a shared culture, as Gellner argued in 1983, to an imagined history and ethnic identity, as Balibar asserted in his 1991 postcolonial critique.

The effort in the United States to place meaning on the developing male is an influential effort to set up terms by which everyone belongs in the nation. Anthony Smith argues that nations must create myths that tie a nation to a geographic location ("Origins of Nations"). We see this connection forged in myths of developing youth, such as that represented by the Boy Scouts of America, that tie boys and young men to a mythologized landscape or an imagined cityscape. Further, the developing male often functions as a metonymy for the progress of a national people, often imagined in crisis. The male is often imagined to be in a state of identity crisis that reflects actual conflicts on a national scene that threaten to destabilize the myth of American exceptionalism that leaders such as Theodore Roosevelt draw on. When the national crisis itself functions as the scene, the man-as-agent is thrown into crisis as well. We see this scene-agent ratio play out in Guy Trebay's *New York Times* article described at the beginning of this chapter. But in response, the developing male is constituted as in a precarious position as an agent, and his identity enables a response to the crisis, through which his masculinity becomes an agency that will ensure the nation remains as great as it historically has been. The ideal national scene is thus reaffirmed by the developing male as an agent, an agent whose actions Americans hope will confirm American exceptionalism. As agents, developing males present both danger and possibility rhetorically as they are imagined to emerge from dependency into a state of legal and economic power from which they can take independent action and engage in the civic sphere.

In fact, the rhetoric of male youth organizations enacts particular constructions of civic engagement for the emergent man. These constructions typically consolidate visions of capitalism and democracy so that the man's democratic engagement is also defined by his participation in the capitalist market economy. We see this blending of democracy with capitalism[2] in the three sites of analysis here. They provide a strong statement about the relationship between constitutive rhetoric and democratic deliberation because they demonstrate that while boys' subjectivity as citizens is being constructed and therefore enabling civic engagement, it is also being limited to the vision that each organization presents. These constructions would demand counternarratives in order to present new possibilities for civic engagement among young males.

And we see possible counternarratives in the ambiguity that arises from the identification process these organizations initiate. Burke argues in *A Grammar of Motives* that ambiguity arises inevitably from identification because the process of identifying is inherently a process of disidentification or division. Here, Burke's rhetorical frame augments and helps explain Smith's ("Origins") and Anderson's conceptions of nationalism as a process of defining an "us" against a "them"—boundaries that do not always align neatly with agents' identities and motives.

This ambiguity ties this project to Omar Swartz's vision of rhetoric as possibility rather than critique, and this approach requires us to understand the complexity of rhetorical identification. Counternarratives are not only possible but also inherent in rhetorical identification, and they are the key to agency. As Burke himself notes in *A Grammar of Motives*, "It is in the areas of ambiguity that transformation takes place" (ix). Yet, while the concept of rhetoric as possibility offers rhetors/subjects agency and space for transformation, Burke does not describe a broadly useful path for the transformation that he locates in ambiguity. Krista Ratcliffe, while noting that discursive ambiguity creates space for a person's agency, rightly warns of the weakness of Burke's take on this transformation, explaining that "Burke's identification demands that differences be bridged. The danger of such a move is that differences and their possibilities, when bridged, may be displaced and mystified" (53). The question of how useful ambiguity might be surfaces in each of the organizations I address in this book. For example, in the incipient Boy Scouts of America, there was ambiguity about the role of militarism in the organization's practices. In promoting civic engagement, founders asked one another, should it teach boys to use weapons, or should it teach them that war is wrong? This ambiguity led to disagreement among them that could have opened up new possibilities for identification as well as *disidentification*—a term Diana Fuss applies to "disavowed" identification (6)—with US citizenship, even transforming the organization's mission into a peace-promoting one, and ultimately contributing to members' civic engagement as antiwar rhetors. The issue, however, remained ambiguous and has been overshadowed historically by the other appeals to citizenship identity the organization offers. As there was no substantial challenge nationally to the organization's construction of the American boy as someone in the process of transforming into a citizen soldier, disidentification did not create transformation. The difference in the founders' conception of the BSA boy was marginalized as an issue, justifying Ratcliffe's warning about the dangers of bridging differences. However, this history does not preclude the possibilities for future transformation.

In shaping the way we imagine the emergent American male and his possibilities for the future, language often directs us toward the past, and this past shapes the scene of American exceptionalism through which citizens identify. The role of the past is central in the rhetorical moves that construct national identity; in fact, Smith argues that our central question should be what role the past plays in creating the present ("Gastronomy" 18). He describes how this works in general terms, focusing on the rhetorical constraints that are enacted:

> [N]ationalists have a vital role to play in the construction of nations, not as culinary artists or social engineers, but as political archaeologists rediscovering and reinterpreting the communal past in order to regenerate the community. Their task is indeed selective—they forget as well as remember the past—but to succeed in their task they must meet certain criteria. Their interpretations must be consonant not only with the ideological demands of nationalism, but also with

the scientific evidence, popular resonance and patterning of particular ethnohistories. ("Gastronomy" 19)

As members of a young country that emerged from a colonial project, people in the United States who identify through nationalism have made use of myths about colonial Europe and the Native Americans whom Europeans colonized. As nationalists, leaders of organizations for boys have shaped these myths around prevailing American scientific and popular conceptions of education, psychology, and economics, among other social narratives. The US Army, for example, places its myth of the emerging soldier in the context of economic mobility.

MASCULINITY AS A HISTORICAL, RHETORICAL CONSTRUCTION IN THE UNITED STATES

Masculinity has taken many forms, sometimes contradictory, and served as a focus of identification for numerous communities that make up a larger national community. In this book, I focus on rhetorical practices of communities that identify with what Connell calls *hegemonic masculinity* (37). Connell's term refers to the strategy of "gender practice" that appears to ensure that men have authority over women (77). The term "name[s] not fixed character types but configurations of practice generated in particular situations in a changing structure of relationships" (81). These configurations can take many forms, including nonlinguistic performance such as dress and language. Because such configurations respond to specific contexts, I situate the rhetorical performances of masculinity in this book within the changing history of economic and social relationships where they have occurred. Connell conceives of masculinity as a project realized through practice over time (72) rather than as a static condition. The hegemony of any form of masculinity exists because it is continually remade through rhetorical acts, with the project of the developing male a key part of this remaking. Typically in the United States, hegemonic masculinity names a practice of manhood among white, straight males who claim authority in the most powerful positions, as well as those who attempt to share in that authority.[3]

As a hegemonic discourse of manhood has evolved during the history of the United States, so have the specific rhetorical practices that define the gendered roles of citizens. From the early nineteenth century to the turn of the twentieth century, the white, male middle class in the United States predominantly defined itself through the gender ideal of manly gentility and respectability. The qualities of manliness were forwarded in popular discourse as characteristics that would build fortunes for aspiring middle-class individuals. As Gail Bederman has described, during most of the nineteenth century, *manliness,* defined as "high-minded self-restraint," was culturally accepted as a dependable way for middle-class men to build wealth (12). This self-restraint was exemplified in men like Andrew Carnegie who attained wealth through what was popularly framed as hard work and self-control. However, Bederman points out that by the 1890s, middle-class manly identity began to stumble because of the changing economy:

> Middle-class manliness had been created in the context of a small-scale, competitive capitalism which had all but disappeared by 1910. Between 1870 and 1910, the proportion of men who were self-employed dropped from 67 percent to 37 percent. . . . Moreover, between 1873 and 1896, a recurring round of severe economic depressions resulted in tens of thousands of bankruptcies and drove home the reality that even a successful, self-denying small businessman might lose everything, unexpectedly and through no fault of his own. (12)

As the middle class saw the decreasing potential for individuals to make fortunes, the discourse of manly restraint lost potency. Moreover, the stage of political and economic power for middle-class men at the turn of the century seemed less solid generally as working-class men threatened to organize and the women's suffrage movement gained steam. White middle-class culture responded with collective anxiety, and as a result the discourse of "masculinity" became a prominent set of arguments for the hegemony of white men. The Boy Scouts of America, the subject of Chapter 2, formed in the first decade of the twentieth century, as this discourse arose.

At the same time that a lifestyle of self-denial became economically and socially unprofitable, it also contradicted the growing cultural identification with leisure that increasingly influenced middle-class men, who expected less from their careers and more from their social lives (Bederman 13). This cultural shift from a discourse of manly restraint to a discourse of masculine leisure and unrestraint was visible in the growing number of recreational and extracurricular organizations for men and boys.

The collective discourse of masculinity that manifested in science, medicine, education, and politics by the turn of the century stressed the physical male body and called on white men to express what was understood as the latent long-forgotten primitive savage in themselves, embracing qualities that, according to this framework, African Americans and others defined as nonwhite (for example, from common immigrant groups) expressed freely as part of their nature. According to this new discourse of American masculinity, white men, who had "naturally" evolved past the savage stage to become civilized, had the evolutionary capacity to control their animal instincts; however, those instincts were latent strengths to be tapped into for power when needed. Literary, gender, and rhetoric scholars have demonstrated some of the practices that make up this discourse (see Bederman; Nelson; Enloe; Rotundo; Mountford). Earlier discourses of manhood throughout the nineteenth century had acknowledged a passionate side to manhood that included lust, greed, and physical assertiveness but represented such qualities as evils to be suppressed (Rotundo 227). At the turn of the twentieth century, however, these qualities were explained as valuable in those who would represent the nation.

While the middle-class culture of white manhood was shifting in reaction to the US economy, science and medicine at the turn of the century in the United States and Europe offered a variety of explanations for masculinity. Over the thirty-year course of his writings, Freud provided a psychoanalytical theory of masculinity, arguing that it was a complex construction with pre-Oedipal roots in the male psyche (Connell 8–10). While positing masculinity as a social construction, Freud also cemented the idea in medical discourse that by adulthood, masculinity is a fixed component of the male makeup.

As Freud theorized about the male mind, others provided evidence for popular theories of the male body. When manly restraint became an ineffectual discursive position, medicine offered discourses of the body to explain why this was so. The concept of "neurasthenia," dubbed "Americanitis" by the Rexall drug company (which offered an elixir for the condition), grew from neurologist George Miller Beard's argument in his 1881 book *American Nervousness*. Beard offered that term for a condition he described as "a lack of nerve force," which he also argued was a condition of civilization. In conceiving of this neurological condition, Beard pitted the intellect against the physical body, arguing that the white, middle-class male, under the work conditions of modern capitalism, had overdeveloped his intellect while his underdeveloped physical body had weakened and become effeminate. The concept of neurasthenia grew from and supported a discourse that positioned white people as more civilized and evolved than people of color. Neurasthenia was a white condition, according to Beard—something that white people experienced because they were the driving force of the capitalist development. Freud contributed to the writings on neurasthenia, focusing on a specific type that he attributed to sexual restraint and abstinence. While Freud and Beard saw the condition as a problem to be overcome, the diagnosis also implicitly confirmed the idea of white people as civilized and people of color as the inverse.

A solution to neurasthenia was offered by psychologist and pedagogy expert G. Stanley Hall, who agreed with Beard that the condition was an inevitable outcome of the way the middle class experienced modernity (Bederman). By drawing on recapitulation theory, Hall proposed that childhood growth stages incorporated the stages of civilized human evolution. The neurasthenic man had failed to cultivate his potential at an important stage in his development by failing to nurture his physical, aggressive impulses during childhood and adolescence. Hall's answer was regimented physical education and activities that would encourage the "savage" in white boys—activities such as sports that demanded embodied competition.

This attention to the body, the fundamental material place from which to approach an otherwise amorphous cultural sense of rapid change and loss of control, provided the site for national rhetorical action, marrying the idea of the boy body to a national cause. While physical education appeared in some schools and recreational organizations in the middle of the nineteenth century, it became nationalized and standardized during the Progressive Era, and promoting regimented, goal-oriented bodily performance became a mainstream approach to reinforcing hegemonic masculinity through the military and military-inspired youth organizations like the BSA. In language that described such bodily performance, organizations for boys called into being a key component of boys' emerging masculine identities.

THE RHETORIC OF MASCULINE TRANSFORMATION IN THREE EXAMPLES

In the next chapter, I argue that in its first years at the turn of the twentieth century, the Boy Scouts of America tapped into the American collective consciousness of race, gender, class, and sexuality to construct the nation as a space in which the American boy occupied a defining role for the ideal citizen. The rhetorical acts occurring in ritualized creeds, the origin story, and myths from the organization's first few years in the United States created a normalizing path to becoming a boy. Informed by a popular scientistic narrative of childhood development of the time, the BSA founders created their own animated narratives of how boys grow mentally and physically into men. As these narratives formed scripts for boys to use in play-acting and performing various organizational rituals, they worked rhetorically to constitute boys' identities as members of the nation, most obviously through terms such as *character, personal prowess, gang instinct,* and *moral courage.* The rhetorical presence of the early BSA can help us to understand the importance of rhetorical appeals more generally in crafting the tie between national consciousness and popular conceptions of boyhood and masculinity during the

Progressive Era. Organizations like the BSA created group experiences in which words worked alongside physical performances such as boys publicly wearing the uniform to constitute boys' civic and national identities in the face of significant ambiguity over the role hegemonic men were to play in the nation at the time.

In Chapter 3, "Constituting American Fraternity Members through the Rhetoric of Becoming," I argue that middle-class males who entered college after high school graduation at midcentury occupied a space that was not typically recognized narratively in American culture as "man" and yet also was recognized as beyond "boy" or "adolescent." This lack of definition left male identity ambiguous for young middle-class white males, many of whom attempted to solidify their hegemonic national position by joining fraternities. Fraternities placed a framework around incipient male adulthood and eased the transition through a narrative that fabricated a tie to ancient Greek history. This college fraternity member identity has been tied to US citizenship through an identity-building rhetoric of democratic engagement. Similar to the other organizations I explore, fraternities typically invoked the genre of origin stories and creeds to constitute identity among their male members. They also invoked racial identification, which they coded through concepts of justice and character. However, mainstream college fraternities were unique because of their emphasis on upward social mobility for their middle-class members. This emphasis on social class identity at a stage when male members were preparing for a career set up an orientation to the marketplace that rewarded upward class mobility and encouraged members to distinguish themselves along class lines. These organizations maintained their original focus on refinement of character in service of genteel manliness that began during the nineteenth century. This chapter demonstrates this process of identification that led to male subjectivity as men-to-be through the example of the Sigma Chi fraternity's handbook and organizational statements. As one of the oldest fraternities in the United States, this organization has been especially attentive to maintaining historical documents that reveal the rhetorical creation of male space by constituting fraternity members' identities through their sense of embodied masculinity through terms such as *brotherhood, commitment,* and *noble values,* along with the term *character* that is employed by all three of the organizations I address. When the contradiction between Sigma Chi's story of "noble values" and the reality of its racially exclusive membership policy is exposed, members attempt to reconcile the contradiction in their public statements.

In Chapter 4, I turn to the use of American manhood rhetoric in more recent history with the case of the US Army's short-running "Army of One" recruitment campaign aimed at recent high school graduates at the turn of the twenty-first century. The US Army represents a rhetorical space from which working-class American boys on the precipice of adulthood can identify as American men, and it represents a bridge between the civic identity formation through schooling that Ian Hunter describes and the spiritual/moral identity formation through extracurricular organizations such as the BSA.

In 2001 the army began its recruiting effort by spending an unprecedented figure to develop a slogan and message. To do so, the army hired the advertising firm Leo Burnett, the creator of McDonald's, Coca-Cola, and Visa campaigns. The firm relied heavily on survey data that identified the high school population's interests, beliefs, and values. The army recruitment campaign that evolved over the next few years employed several modes of communication to broadcast its appeal to youth identity, including brochures handed out by army representatives in recruiting offices and at recruiting events held at places of business, high schools, and college campuses. Despite these efforts, the campaign lasted only five years, far briefer than the prior twenty-year "Be All That You Can Be" campaign.

By pairing text with images in recruiting documents, the army attempted to constitute a primarily male youth identity through the Soldier's Creed and the army uniform. These images and texts reveal an underlying narrative appeal to personal transformation, from what it portrayed as a directionless boy in search of an identity to a directed, self-possessed, and productive man in the army. The campaign points to the range of ways in which constitutive rhetorics of the American boy have been used to build collective and individual national masculine identity. In this case, the army's attempt to create a transitional identity of "becoming" based on a perception of young males' values was attended by unreconciled ambiguity between the national boy and the national man in the army's campaign, as well as by the civic/moral divide, both of which the army attempted to bridge with visual images of a soldier who encompasses both elements of male development. This is perhaps the most obvious example among the three examples of an organization's attempt to create national masculinity identification among males. Unique among the organizations I investigate here, the army targeted males of color along with white males.

In Chapter 5, I outline a possible pedagogical approach and course organization that could result from the ideas discussed in this monograph. Based on my own teaching practices over several years incorporating sites of analysis local to my undergraduate and graduate students, I suggest an approach to exploring emergent masculine identity with students at a range of levels. Finally, I connect the case analyses of organizations to lingering contemporary questions about the role of rhetoric in constructing American males as masculine American men, and I explore possibilities for those questions to inform our composition and rhetoric pedagogy. As manhood progresses in the face of the evolving gender politics and capitalism of the early twenty-first century, I suggest that bringing sites of collective masculine, national identity into rhetoric and writing classrooms can help students examine the terms through which we construct civic engagement and personal identity, terms that tend to obscure how power is exchanged. Issues of national identity and gender affect young hegemonically identified males, but also the spectrum of gendered students who do not fit the performance scripts that these organizations put forth.

2

The Rhetorical Performance of Masculine Transformation in the Boy Scouts of America in the Early Twentieth Century

> It would have been impossible to have attracted, enrolled and trained over a third of a million men and over a million boys each year—out of every part of the United States[—]without making those communities, their institutions, their community chests, their newspapers, and their homes, more boy-minded.
> —William D. Murray, *The History of the Boy Scouts of America,* 1937

LOOKING AT THE BOY SCOUTS OF AMERICA THROUGH A RHETORICAL LENS

IN THE NATIONAL SCOUTING MUSEUM in Irving, Texas, a floor-to-ceiling placard explains to visitors the story of how Scouting came to the United States:

> The year was 1909. American publisher William D. Boyce found himself lost on the streets of London in a dense fog. As he pondered his next move, a Scout emerged from the mist. He offered to take Boyce to his destination and the man gladly accepted.
>
> When their journey had come to an end, the American reached into his pocket to give the Scout a coin for his efforts. The young man stopped him, courteously explaining that he was a Scout and would not accept payment for doing his duty.

This story has been repeated many times, often increasing in detail in the years since the founding of the Boy Scouts of America (BSA) in 1910,[1] as William D. Boyce and other founding members transformed the British concept of Scouting into an American organization primed to the national hegemonic imaginary, with its ideologically loaded set of cultural beliefs. The following more colorful version is from the 1984 children's book *The Boy Scouts: An American Adventure*:

> The British capital lay in the grip of a dense "pea soup" fog. It had rolled in during the night and had enveloped the whole city in its smoky yellowness. Street lamps had been lit before noon. They shone with a feeble glow that penetrated only a few feet into the murkiness.
>
> An American businessman walking slowly along the poorly lit street stopped under a lamp post and tried to orient himself. No doubt now, he was lost.
>
> The figure of a boy moved past the man, then turned and came back.
>
> "Can I help you, sir?" the youngster asked.
>
> "You certainly can," said the man. "I have a business appointment somewhere around here. I'll be much obliged if you'll tell me how to get there."
>
> "If you'll give me the address I'll take you there."
>
> When they got to the destination, Mr. Boyce reached into his pocket for a tip. But the boy stopped him.
>
> "No thank you, sir. I won't take anything for helping."
>
> "And why not?" the American asked.
>
> "Because I'm a Scout! Haven't you heard about Baden-Powell's Boy Scouts?"
>
> The American had not. "Tell me about them," he said.
>
> The boy told him what he could of himself and his brother Scouts and all the fun they were having in Scouting.
>
> But the American wanted to know still more.
>
> "I know where you can find out," said the boy. "Our headquarters is close by, in [sic] Victoria Street. The General may even be in the office today."

"The General?"

"Baden-Powell himself, sir." "Fine," said the American. "Let me finish my errand. Then, if you have time, we'll go to your headquarters."

The boy waited, then showed the way to the Scout office, and disappeared before the American had a chance to learn his name. (Peterson)

The persistence of this story as it evolved points to its rhetorical power. We see in these two versions two descriptions that, to return to Burke, "place a person in his own eyes, as he surrounds himself with a scene which, he is assured, attests to his moral quality. For he can feel that he participates in the quality that the scene itself is thought to possess" (qtd. in Clark 3).

To ask the rhetorician's questions, then, of what it means to make a community and a home "boy-minded," and how such a transformation is presented, is also to ask how readers of this origin story are placed within it. And to read such a story through a Burkean lens is to see the formation of the Boy Scouts of America as a phenomenon of identification, wherein readers imagine themselves as like the agents acting within the scene that is constructed. Such a view helps us to understand how this site of rhetoric has had the power to help shape gendered national consciousness. Significantly, evidence suggests that the events of the story actually did not happen this way. As I explain in more detail later in this chapter, the story is based on a set of related events that have become elaborated on to form an origin myth. The myth has thrived because of its ability to reach its audience and create in them an identity that is tied to a broader national scene. The boy character in the story is anonymous, so he could be any boy. He is brave—he can guide a stranger through a fog; he is a leader—he can help a foreigner who is lost. He is in control. He can be counted on in hard times. Perhaps most important, he is not motivated extrinsically by money (he refuses a tip) but intrinsically by a sense of duty to a higher calling, framed by his membership in a national institution. In refusing a tip, the boy is positioned as an alternative to the Protestant, money-seeking, self-made American man at a historical moment when that myth was losing some of its earlier currency. This character is above the monetary measure of his value and sees in himself as an individual and in the nation a transcendent sense of "right." One could say, using the language of Burke's dramatistic framework, that his act contains the scene. That is, his actions direct the audience to understand his nation as a place where "character" is valued above material reward. This statement about character is a significant rhetorical move toward a boy reader's fledgling middle-class national identity, an identity that must wrestle with the ambiguity between the demand of the capitalist market that a person work hard in order to achieve material success and the reality that participation in American capitalism does not guarantee that success. That this tale has survived from its origins in 1911 to the present—even prompting a statue, "The Unknown Scout," in its honor gifted to the British in 1926—is evidence of its ability to reconcile this ambiguity in American national identity.

The often-cited Unknown Scout story belies the rhetorical aims of the organizers at the BSA's inception. To look at this project historically is to encounter rhetoric at the complex intersections of economy, gender, and race during the first decade of the twentieth century in the United States, at a point of competing discourses. The language of the American Boy Scout movement was part of a Progressive Era masculinist project of imagining the nation and its relationship to classed, raced, and gendered bodies by mediating middle-class boys' consciousness through stories about difference. This mediation happened through targeted appeals such as the BSA origin story and the Scout Oath—both of which would become mundane but important as often-repeated gestures of identification—and through less mundane means such as the organization's national charter.

The Boy Scouts of America was able to gain such immediate and strong cultural and state support, I argue, because its language and other symbols, along with its practices, effectively persuaded boys and their parents that membership was part of proper male citizenship grooming—in other words, a way to understand and traverse the boundary between boyhood and manhood. This citizenship grooming was presented as a natural desire of boys of good character and their parents. As we see in Boy Scout practices, the organization did not attempt to persuade boys of these beliefs through direct public appeals to credibility, emotion, or data. Rather, they appealed through common rituals that tapped into boys' consciousness, shaping their identities and hailing them as incipient members of the nation who would identify primarily as Americans through the fog of class antagonism, who would resolve the problem of individualism that remained in tension with national unity, and who would symbolically forward national imperialist expansion despite the controversial attendant violence. Viewing the early BSA through a Burkean framework reveals the importance of identification in crafting the tie between national consciousness and the developing boy during this era.

In this chapter, I consider the Boy Scouts of America as a rhetorical site, using Burke's framework for understanding identification as a socializing force. Burke's dramatistic categories explain how language enacts motives, how one performs persuasion and motivates others to participate in the performance, transforming a situation. For Burke, rhetoric is the use of language to influence attitudes and actions. With its treatment of rhetoric as identification, Burke's rhetorical theory helps us to understand how and why people participate in a cause such as a youth movement based on myths like that of the Unknown Scout. Burke's system is particularly useful for explaining stories like the BSA origin myth because his pentad is concerned not with "forms of experience" but rather with "forms of talk about experience," though he does see experience and language as interrelated (Bizzell and Herzberg). As intently as the early Boy Scout movement focused on physical development and the performative experience of American boys, it was most significantly a movement of talk about experience. It is this talk that can help us understand the enduring weight of this organization in US culture.

The BSA offered boys several overlapping identities, including racial, class, ethnic, religious, cultural, urban and rural, pro-military and nonviolent, with sexuality a mostly unspoken but present category in the early twentieth century. Rather than directly addressing these social identities and lived realities, the early BSA presented the Boy Scout identity as one that could subsume all others for boys and thus incorporate them into an identity as ideal American agents. However, the project of identity is always incomplete, and as Burke emphasizes, rife with ambiguity. Such ambiguity emerged regularly in national conversations within and about the BSA. These ambiguities were sometimes reconciled politically by the organization's early leaders in response to specific questions about immediate courses of action, such as whether boys should carry handguns or whether African American boys should be allowed to join troops with white boys. Sometimes identity ambiguity was addressed locally, as when individual troops were established for boys who did not fit the mainstream national profile, such as the small number of African American troops in the South. These kinds of national and local responses could have broadened the national narrative of the BSA, but the handbook and other standardizing documents have largely remained unchanged, ensuring that ambiguity has continued and that the project of grooming boys to become men has measured all boys against the hegemonic definition of masculinity metaphorized in those documents. In failing to resolve the ambiguity in its definition of the ideal man-in-the-making by revising its narratives, the Boy Scouts has been a conservative organization and encouraged a conservative identity performance among members, despite the diverse, sometimes progressive goals the organization began with. Such refusal to reimagine its foundational documents, and thus to create new possibilities for identity performance, ties the BSA to the other organizations discussed in this book, each of which has maintained its hegemonic masculine narrative through similar ambiguity. The Boy Scouts set a pattern of imagining the young American male that both creates a paradigm and ensures that the organizations themselves will lose members as their metaphors for masculinity remain static while those of the larger US culture evolve.

THE BRITISH BOY SCOUTS AND THE
RHETORICAL ORIGINS OF THE BSA

If, as rhetorician Maurice Charland argues, "one cannot exist but as a subject within a narrative" (141), and the subject of the BSA myth is one that its "rhetoric both addresses and leads to come to be," then the BSA constituted its audience as subject, and in this case, one with a representative national identity and loyalty. The BSA constructed far-reaching, hegemonic ideals about male character and the central national function of its boys by creating its self-conscious subjects through performance that its boys enacted. These ideals were communicated through several means, including the Scouting handbook that describes the ritualized performances boys are to enact.

Before exploring these performances within the United States, it is important to note that American manly subjective consciousness is rooted much further back historically than the specific sites I analyze in this chapter. It was built in part on British concepts of citizenship and colonial subjectivity. The progenitor of the BSA, the British Boy Scouts, formed in response to a perceived crisis in the innate characters of the men who served in the British colonial armies. The Boer War in particular and Britain's failures there prompted British army leaders to question their soldiers' strength of character. Searching for something fixable to blame for their defeat, they funneled their insecurity into questioning whether their soldiers possessed the bravery required to maintain the Empire (Enloe 49). Lieutenant General Lord Baden-Powell, who would go on to form the British Scouts, argued that the soldiers under his command during this time "lacked fundamental character values, such as dependability, initiative and resourcefulness" and that "their attitude and outlook on life was such that figuratively, they expected to be tucked in at night" (Murray 2). His language suggested that the soldiers were both incomplete men and on their way to becoming neurasthenic, as so many upper-class men were imagined to have become during that time in Britain, and that they were in no position to defend the nation against the threat of the colonized Other whom they were sent to restrain. In fact, "[t]hey had not been subjected to those necessities of life which bring out the qualities which humans have when given proper opportunity and when stimulated by proper leadership" (Murray 2). In addition, Baden-Powell shared British imperialists' fears that venereal disease, racial intermarriage, and declining birthrates were endangering Britain's international power (Enloe 50). He addressed these fears by participating in a discourse on the British male character.

In service to the British nation, Baden-Powell developed a handbook in 1899 for soldiers to use to gain those "fundamental character values" he found lacking in them. The handbook, *Aids to Scouting,* became popular and was adopted by schools for boys in England. He later wrote *Rovering to Success*, a book of advice for older Scouts. Both publications were informed by colonial understandings of race, civilization, and manhood. For example, one illustration in *Rovering to Success* distinguishes between Baden-Powell's ideal of a "white man" (drawn as tall, muscular, and standing upright at attention) and a "man" (drawn as short and dark-skinned, in wrinkled clothes) (104). Despite this colonial ideal, he found that "the ordinary boy in civilized countries" did not measure up. He argues,

> We badly need some . . . training for our lads if we are to keep up manliness in our race instead of lapsing into a soft and sloppy, [sic] nation. That is why I say that if you choose to prepare yourself for success as I suggest . . . . you will not only be doing yourself good, but you will be doing a good thing for the country, "You'll be a MAN, my son," and you will thus be making one more *man* for the nation. (22)

Baden-Powell's publications were a rhetorical response to British imperial ideologies and fears of the Empire's demise. Placing the source of British colonial success or failure in the hands of white British boys, and using racialized images of men to make concrete the distinction between success and failure, Baden-Powell congealed these ideologies into an argument for the way the state and parents should groom white British boys. His first book for boys, *Scouting for Boys,* was published in 1908, in the midst of several education reform acts in England and Wales that made education accessible for poor Britons. In the book, Baden-Powell stresses cooperation and mutual respect among boys across social classes, suggesting a broad potential for Scouting.

Responding to encouragement from schools and his friends, Baden-Powell drew from work on the British Young Men's Christian Association (YMCA) to form a set of guidelines that led to the formalization of the Boy Scouts organization in 1908, the same year he published *Scouting for Boys.* The Boy Scouts soon developed distinctive features, including the Oath or Promise; the motto, "Be Prepared"; the "Daily Good Turn"; the uniform; the badge; and the Scout Law (9–10). The first uniforms looked like Baden-Powell's uniform from the South African Constabulary (10). The Law included twelve parts: A Scout is Trustworthy, A Scout is Loyal, A Scout is Helpful, A Scout is Friendly, A Scout is Courteous, A Scout is Kind, A Scout is Obedient, A Scout is Cheerful, A Scout is Thrifty, A Scout is Brave, a Scout is Clean, and A Scout is Reverent. These concrete features, representations of a broad national ideology, would influence the Boy Scouts in the United States.

In 1910, William D. Boyce, an American publisher from Chicago, formed the Boy Scouts of America. The BSA adopted laws and practices that were modeled after those of the British Boy Scouts but that developed over the next several years to reflect and codify American national values. While several organizations for boys existed during this period, including the American Boy Scouts, Boy Scouts of the United States, Sons of Daniel Boone, and Boy Pioneers of America, these organizations emphasized military training. Through the BSA, Boyce intended to promote citizenship training for boys above all (Petterchak 67). In doing so, he would have to work out what citizenship training meant and persuade boys that it was worthwhile.

According to apocryphal accounts in the National Scouting Museum, in Murray's history of the BSA, and on numerous official and unofficial BSA organizational websites, Boyce met a British

Boy Scout by chance on a business trip in England. As we saw in the account at the beginning of this chapter, performing a "good turn," the "Unknown Scout" helped him find his way through a London fog, and Boyce was so impressed that he met with Baden-Powell to learn all he could about the organization. Historical records show that Boyce in fact stopped in London on his way to an African safari and went to Baden-Powell's headquarters, but he did not actually meet with Baden-Powell himself (Petterchak 63–64). The letters in which Boyce recounts this story contain no mention of fog (Rowan 27–28), and weather reports from the *London Times* indicate there was no fog during Boyce's visit (58). The fog element may have been added later in 1911, after an incident that year in Rhode Island when a man who was lost in a fog was helped by a Boy Scout who refused a cash tip (58).

While this origin myth of the BSA served a practical function by simplifying a complex and banal history of mergers among smaller US organizations for boys and rivalries among founding members, it also provided a rhetorical template for the ideal Boy Scout, functioning (for my purposes) as a vehicle for Burkean identification—with an ideal, unknown boy figure and with a guide for the ideal blending of mind and body, directed toward national good, that would reshape a boy into a man. The story calls on its audience of boys to employ what Charland calls "follow[ing] narrative consistency and the motives through which they are constituted as audience members" (147). Such elements of identification are rhetorical, Charland argues, because they "induce human cooperation" through discursive effects (133). His claim here is Burkean, but with a twist: rather than accepting what he sees as Burke's humanist assumption that audience members are agents free to choose how they identify, Charland weaves into identification Althusser's assertion that social subjects are themselves constructed through ideology. Through rhetorical effects, Charland argues, subjects are those who at the same moment speak their subjectivity and introduce action (133). In other words, through the persuasive effects of words, a subject receives an identity from others and uses that identity to persuade others. In the case of the BSA, boys became subjects who promoted the boy ideal even as they may not have lived it entirely.

In the Burkean rhetorical scene of the Boy Scouts, a boy is induced to become conscious of himself as a male citizen-in-the-making, and as long as he acts as an ideal citizen, there is consistency between the scene and the act. However, this identification process is full of potential ambiguity, as it is modeled on an ideal of hegemonic masculinity rather than reality. In imagining an ideal male citizen, the identification narrative set up boundaries that excluded some males (and, obviously, females) and encouraged others to live with an identity that conflicted with other racial, sexual, political, and class-based identities. Yet the Unknown Scout story has worked for many as constitutive rhetoric because it presents the unknown boy's practical *action* as a statement about his character, and that action-based statement is a crucial element of male identity in the United States. In this case, the boy's actions represent something innate about him rather than a concrete political, racial, or sexual marker, though a boy's physical being also played a crucial role in his character in the paradigm to which the Boy Scouts subscribed. While they were imagined, both the intangible and the physical characteristics of the ideal Boy Scout emerged from larger cultural currents in the United States at the turn of the twentieth century.

During the last two decades of the nineteenth century and the first two of the twentieth, the United States was in the process of imagining itself as a nation responding to perceived overlapping social crises that threatened the established race and class hegemony. Beyond the United States, the West had understood its dominant political and cultural position in the mid-nineteenth century through science-based ideas about the origin of races (Bhabha 246). This narrative of inherent dominance worked through external colonialism for Europe and internal colonialism for the United States; by the end of the nineteenth century, however, the United States faced a shift toward international dominance and colonial opportunity as well as a growing domestic instability in class, race, and gender hierarchies. Americans began to reimagine their role in the nation through new language and practices that redefined race along with gender and class, effectively reinscribing who and how ideal members of the nation should be and behave. Once slavery ended as a legally sanctioned practice and African Americans gained legal access, however fraught, to social and economic power, the growing presence of large numbers of immigrants from southern Europe and Ireland complicated the racial landscape; on another front, the women's suffrage movement gained momentum. In the face of these threats, new rhetoric and discourse developed among the government administration and the middle class that reinscribed white manhood as the ideal representation of a nation.

In response to this shifting social structure, the public rhetorical performances aimed at boys played a key role, establishing patterns of thought and enforcing values that calibrated the young male body to an imagined community of potential citizens, soldiers, and workers. This calibration was designed to persuade boys of their identities: retold stories, organized rituals, and daily habits constituted a consciousness through which young boys could embody national subjectivity. The rhetorical practices of the early Boy Scouts of America helped solidify national ideology in the homes of mainstream Americans by offering a rhetorical bridge between developing youth, parents, and institutions.

In this chapter, when I refer to the ideal Scout, I refer to a hegemonic masculine identity that Scouting promoted, coding the Boy Scout as white, heterosexual, Christian, and middle class. While the BSA officially allowed straight boys from all classes, religions, and races to participate in Scouting, the image of the ideal Scout was consistently presented as white, Christian, and middle class. The British colonial narratives that informed BSA practices also tied Scouting to whiteness and national power. While troops across the United States included boys in a range of race and religion categories, the Scout as he was presented rhetorically was hegemonically masculine, meaning white and heterosexual.

The story of William D. Boyce's first encounter with the Boy Scouts in England, wherein he was rescued from a treacherous fog in a foreign land by a British Boy Scout, created one template for the BSA's rhetorical performances, making the presence of US Scouts into a symbol of the prowess of the nation. Through this symbol and the performance of rituals that accompanied membership in the BSA, boys were prompted to understand themselves as embodying character traits that aligned with imagined ideal national character traits. Their audiences—including parents, other youth, BSA leaders, union leaders, and others who came into contact with the public performance of Scouting—were persuaded to imagine a community in which boys represented national values such as thrift and physically conditioned male bodies.

This performative relationship between boys, the ideas they represented, and the communities for whom they performed constitutes a Burkean scene-act-agent ratio. The dramatistic rhetorical model I outline in Chapter 1 provides a framework for explaining the way embodied performance functions rhetorically, and also helps demonstrate how the boys themselves were persuaded by their performances. Through examining the textual performances of the early Boy Scout movement, we can better understand the role of youth organization rhetoric in navigating the complex, contradictory mainstream values at the turn of the twentieth century, rhetoric that responded to the discourse of hegemonic white masculinity. Moreover, we can understand these narratives and practices as rhetorical performances of nationalism that blended body and idea to form an embodied national rhetoric that persists.

THE ROLE OF THE BOY SCOUTS OF AMERICA
IN CULTIVATING MASCULINITY

The Boy Scout organization, which began in Britain in 1908, grew from a discourse of manly restraint (Enloe), but the Boy Scout movement in the United States that followed in 1909 developed through the discourse of masculinity, focusing on physicality and sporting activities that would fill middle-class Americans' leisure time. As dominant national discourse changed the expected behaviors of white men to accommodate the physicality of masculinity, it followed that mainstream-minded parents would raise boys differently. The only alternative this narrative offered parents was that their boys would grow to be men who were unable to control their physical impulses, or men who were effeminate or physically ill, unable to tap into these physical impulses when necessary—effectively, not real men. The implied logical end of such failure to behave according to national norms was that the nation would suffer because African Americans and women would gain hegemony, and civilization would give way to savagery. But parents were probably more immediately attracted to the BSA for its mundane offerings of daily practices and guidance—a bridge between formal schooling, religious practice, and home life. The BSA promised boys character-building activities that would mediate the relationship between a boy as an individual and society at large, imagined as a national community. With the activities the BSA cultivated as habits of mind and body, the BSA would form future complete citizens who had internalized their roles as national representatives, including representing growing corporate capitalism and middle-class consumption.

The founders and advocates of the American Boy Scouts framed BSA activities as a collection of actions and attitudes that turned on crafting the proper relationship between body and character. This relationship was developed through private and public rhetoric that persuaded boys that they should become, and could become, a particular kind of citizen-male that was synonymous with American personhood, and that they were part of an inherently superior national calling. As boys performed Scouting, they in turn persuaded their onlookers of these things.

The incipient Boy Scouts of America was endorsed by President Roosevelt and followed the birth of physical education classes in public schools during that first decade in the new century. Psychologists and educators theorized that parents should encourage the savage in their boys so that the boys would grow into strong men, able to control their wild instincts but to call on them when necessary. Organizations like the YMCA, which made its way to the United States in 1851, played a key role in overseeing boys' physical development and encouraging their spiritual development. However, the rhetoric of the BSA was more focused than the rhetoric of the YMCA, which was and remains a relatively loose association of community organizations and ideologies.

As the organization developed in the United States under the direction of William D. Boyce, it maintained much of the symbolism from the British Boy Scouts but functioned as a tool for building American middle-class nationalism. That the early BSA was middle class in its ideology and orientation to mainstream American culture is suggested in the makeup of Scout leaders, or "Scouters," during this time. Data from early Scout leaders' applications show that most were middle class (Hantover 191–92). And though officially an organization for boys of all colors, classes, and religions, the BSA drew from the discourse of white supremacy and colonialism to propel boys toward its goal of crafting male citizens. Thus the organization represents a paradox in nationalism during this time: it both welcomed boys from a variety of backgrounds and presented them with a discourse of hierarchical racial evolution in service of its decidedly middle-class goals.

THE INFLUENCE OF THEODORE ROOSEVELT AND MILITARISM ON BSA RHETORICAL STRATEGIES

Perhaps the element of the early BSA that most effectively extended its potential to inspire identification was its hero figure or idealized agent. In England the Boy Scouts had a perfect model of civilized masculinity in the colonial figure of Baden-Powell. In the United States, that representative figure became former president Theodore Roosevelt. Roosevelt was a symbol of new national manhood as president even before the formation of the BSA in 1910. As middle-class American men's attention turned to masculinity, Roosevelt demonstrated how race worked in claiming male power (Bederman). He encouraged men to take up the "white man's burden" through his stories of conquering the Indians, his prior involvement in the Spanish-American war, and his race-based anti-immigration policy for the Japanese. His eleven-month safari to Africa became the inspiration for the sensational adventure stories he wrote, constructing himself as the civilized white superior to savage natives. They also portrayed him as tapping into his own savage evolutionary history. In these stories, Africa was constructed as masculine space through the figure of the primal African rapist. In accounts of Africa as a safari destination, Roosevelt's writings showed Africa to be a place where "the white man could prove his superior manhood by reliving the primitive, masculine life of his most distant evolutionary forefathers" (Bederman 215). His account would work as a model for BSA activities.

As with Baden-Powell, Roosevelt's efforts to cultivate masculinity among his nation's citizens stemmed from his interest in military strength, beginning during his presidency from 1901 to 1909 and his goal of reforming the military in order to build the country into an imperial power. The Spanish-American War created a new empire for the United States, and Roosevelt expanded and reformed the military to control the new territory. His reforms included putting younger men in positions of authority within the military to reflect his emphasis on physical ability, in contrast to the prior practice of placing more seasoned officers in command, based primarily on their experience and wisdom. He also imposed an annual fitness test for officers in the army and the navy (Oyos, "Congress").

Roosevelt's goal was not as simple as political control of new territories through physical force. He saw the military as a vehicle to enable the United States to compete for international markets, a goal that he framed as "spread[ing] the benefits of their unique civilization" (Oyos, "Theodore Roosevelt, Congress"). His strategy for making a persuasive claim for this economic development was to assume the ideologies of race constructed by British colonial leaders, leading his audience to identify with what he posited as the superiority of white Europeans. He began his 1909 speech "The Expansion of the White Races" by proclaiming that

> [t]here is one feature in the expansion of the peoples of white, or European, blood during the past four centuries which should never be lost sight of, especially by those who denounce such expansion on moral grounds. On the whole, the movement has been fraught with lasting benefit to most of the peoples already dwelling in the lands over which the expansion took place.

So while the expansionist goals were largely economic, Roosevelt framed them in terms of racial character, just as the BSA would frame its goals. The ratio of the scene, in which white Europeans and those of European descent were superior, to the agent—whites—explained US military intervention in the Philippines and Latin America as a reasonable action.

Furthermore, Roosevelt seemed to believe that foreign and military policies would shape the national character of the United States (Oyos, "Theodore Roosevelt and the Implements" 635). The Boy Scouts became a post-presidential term extension of Roosevelt's imperialist mission: once the Boy Scouts of America officially organized, he confirmed the connection between the Scouts and the nation by publicly supporting the organization. Roosevelt certainly influenced BSA founding member William D. Murray, who invoked Roosevelt as a model in his description of the great benefit the Scouts have offered to the health of boys:

> The outdoor life in particular has brought to the Scout health values important in the development of the race, but lost to increasing thousands, because of our having so much of the indoor and sedentary in modern life. . . . President Theodore Roosevelt, as a young man, built his puny body into a strong one by this very formula, and in adult life frequently referred to these values which Scouting made available to its boys. (217)

In addition to such public references, the myth of Roosevelt surfaced in the official goals of the Boy Scouts, as it did in the comic tales of Roosevelt's adventures, and the Scouts' connection to Roosevelt is remembered through the organization's rituals. For example, since Roosevelt's death in 1919, Scouts have planted trees in his honor and made annual pilgrimages to his grave (Murray 152). That same year, the Scouts adopted a resolution honoring Roosevelt as a leader and role model. And Roosevelt himself praised the Boy Scouts publicly:

> I believe in work and I believe in play; I believe in drudgery when drudgery is necessary; and in love of adventure also. Above all, I believe that the American citizen of the future should be brave and hardy, that he should possess also the personal prowess, and that he should also possess the spirit

which puts personal prowess at the service of the Commonwealth; which is another way of saying that he must be law-
abiding, and have consideration for the rights and the feelings
of others. The Boys Scout Movement is pre-eminently successful along all of these different lines. (qtd. in Murray 243)

The ideas of being "brave and hardy" and having "personal prowess" are consistent with the early-twentieth-century concept of masculinity I describe in Chapter 1. In the context of Roosevelt's public
persona, these were the qualities that led him on his adventure in
Africa (which replicated the colonial adventures of Baden-Powell
in Africa but also carried nostalgia for popular tales like Kipling's
The Jungle Book). But in Roosevelt's statement, these qualities are
subordinated to "the spirit which puts [them] at the service of the
Commonwealth." This "spirit" ties a Scout to a perception of the
nation as a system of laws and a space in which he imagines himself
existing along with others he hasn't met, as part of an imagined
community (as theorized by Benedict Anderson). "Spirit" is also
a metaphor for the restraining element that harnesses boys' bur-
geoning masculinity to the imagined nation rather than to various
social factions that were growing at the time. Spirit is, in other
words, Burkean agency. It was a vague quality a boy could achieve
in order to become part of the nation. Because this spirit is intangible, it is not something that can be measured in dollars earned or
saved. By juxtaposing the nation with the need for personal prowess
and physical conditioning, Roosevelt characterizes the nation as a
space—a scene—akin to the jungle he has described in his mythi-
cal accounts. The scene he conjures is one in which there are those
who can lead the rest of us through an uncivilized morass toward
civilization—and boys can become those leaders.

The activities of Boy Scouts centered on achieving this spirit by
mastering such skills as orienteering and other wilderness survival
techniques. These skills were to be applied in service of the nation,
and in public myth that meant helping elderly women cross the
street or helping travelers find their way in a fog; in other words,
common citizens would benefit from the Scouts. Yet the rhetoric
of the Scouts as a whole and particularly the narratives used to en-

courage boys' interests in Scouting recall the narrative of jungle adventure rather than of everyday urban or rural American life. Again, the scene is the jungle, whether imagined as wild in Africa or as concrete in the urban United States. Between these very different scenes the organization creates—everyday American life (even imaginary) and dangerous jungle—there is an ambiguity of purpose.

The colonial narrative that underlies many of the practices and values of the Boy Scouts sometimes pulls directly from the most fantastic of British colonial narratives of the late nineteenth century. Rudyard Kipling's *The Jungle Book* serves as a backdrop in handbooks to explain Boy Scouts principles. For example, the Cub Scouts, which is a branch of the Boy Scouts for boys younger than age twelve, requires members to earn a Bobcat badge. The bobcat is the American version of the panther, an animal featured as a character in *The Jungle Book*. This story is explained to potential Cubs at the beginning of the "Bear" handbook to teach a moral: "Mowgli had learned to live as a wolf cub and had begun to learn the wisdom of the bear, but he needed older friends to teach him things that would protect him. Like Mowgli, you can call on parents and leaders to help you" (Boy Scouts of America [BSA] 14). Mowgli, readers may remember from the story, is an orphaned white English child left to live in the jungle in India. He is adopted by a band of animals who meet once a month to take care of governance of their group. Their enemy is the "monkey people" (BSA 13), a group of monkeys that provides a thinly veiled metaphor for Indians. Boys today enact a scene from *The Jungle Book* as a ceremony when they receive the Wolf badge, and parts of the story are integrated into several other ceremonies (Dunn).

When the story was told in the United States during the BSA's early years, Scouts could easily picture the popular tale because the content was supported by the US history of race relations and the popular adulation for Roosevelt and his travels in the African jungle, also featured elsewhere in BSA literature. Though readers today may experience the story more as a Disneyesque tale than a comment on civilization, it is important to understand that during the late nineteenth and early twentieth centuries, Americans were engrossed in stories of Roosevelt's travels and stories like *The Jungle Book* and *Tarzan of the Apes*. Importantly, science during this time was fixated on explaining civilization and its gradations through colonial models. Scientific myths like "neurasthenia"[2] worked in tandem with an abundance of hypotheses on the biological foundations of race and civilization.[3] Kipling himself published the poem "The White Man's Burden" in 1901, dedicating it to Roosevelt for encouraging the United States to colonize the Philippines (Kaplan 13), reducing the colonized and potentially colonized to "new-caught, sullen peoples, Half-devil and half-child" (qtd. in Bederman 187). Roosevelt acknowledged the poem as "poor poetry but good sense from the expansionist standpoint" (qtd. in Bederman 187). In this environment, *The Jungle Book*'s white audiences were likely to find in the story truisms about "civilization" and their place within it that supported the scene the BSA created, and using this scene, the BSA painted the transition from boyhood to manhood as a process of gaining national and racial power.

THE BOY SCOUTS AND EXPERIENTIAL RHETORIC: THE BODY IN SCENE, ACT, AND AGENT

The background of the BSA describes the national cultural and economic scene in which Boy Scouts enacted their roles. The Scouts as actors were a reflection of Boyce's story of finding his way in the fog. Boys were to act like the British boy in the story while helping lost Americans find their way through a cultural fog in which the pathway to economic success was uncertain, the hegemonic status of white men needed to be shored up, and the future for boys was seen as a brave new world. The certainty of rituals and uniforms provided a way to perform strength—a show of unity of a selected, tested group of future middle-class citizens, the act that would be contained by the scene.

The Boy Scouts, as an American organization, was not simply a connected series of troops across the nation within which boys could develop their characters and attain a particular set of skills privately. The activities of the boys, though described as building inner fortitude, were routinely directed outward as performances for larger American audiences. Boy Scouts were groomed to "Scout" publicly, to be seen "Scouting." *Scouting* magazine articulated this effort to make the symbolic a more tangible source of identification in 1919 when it claimed, "The Boy Scout movement is as near concrete as an idea can be" (Hunt). In materializing the nebulous concept of Scouting, boys gave embodied performances that generated the "talk about" national boyhood and manhood that is the organization's most important effect. Embodied acts such as wearing the uniform in public were performative statements of what it meant to Scout, demonstrating to audiences and boy performers themselves that the American man was alive and integral to national success.

The Boy Scout Uniform as a Persuasive Embodied Experience

Not all versions of the Scouts' origin story offer an explanation for how Boyce knew the Unknown Scout was a Boy Scout, but in illustrations that accompany the story, the boy typically wears a Scout uniform. Its various audiences are guided to experience the story as a mystery (How did the boy find Boyce in the fog and guide him? Who was this unknown boy?) and as an account of a boy who executed the kind of brave leadership that Roosevelt and other brave men were fabled to exhibit in Africa and other foreign lands. The ethereal quality of the story directs audiences' attention to intangible, timeless concepts of masculine character. This mysterious young boy acted as a leader in the presence of a grown man who was lost.

The Unknown Scout parable and others were enacted through BSA ceremonial practices and through the bodies of the early Scouts when they wore their uniforms. The talk about the uniforms from that era suggests that organizers were somewhat conscious of the rhetorical effect the costume had on boys. MacDonald claims that uniforms were liberating for the first Scouts, providing a symbolic contrast to the social expectations that a boy be "buttoned up, stifled in heavy clothes, and too often under orders to behave himself" (6). Once in uniform, Scouts could "play the exciting game of 'man-hunting' under the leadership of the most charismatic hero of the day" (6). Murray too concludes that the uniform played an "important educational part" (164) in Scouting. This importance would, a couple of decades later, be starkly underlined in an official message to Scouts in the organization's October 1930 merchandise catalog:

> The Scout Uniform is a part of the romance of Scouting. It is a symbol of the ideals and outdoor activities for which the Movement stands. It has the picturesque touch which helps the Scout identify himself with the great traditions of our outdoorsmen—the pioneer, explorer, scout, and cowboy—which underlie the psychology of Scouting. Here in America, as throughout the world, the Scout Uniform has earned the respect of the general public. It is one of the significant and important features of the Boy Scout Movement, because of its definite educational value to the boy himself, to the Scout Leader, to the Patrol, to the Troop and the community. (qtd. in Murray 164)

The catalog suggests that the inherent value of the uniform is self-evident and far-reaching because it conveys a narrative to anyone who sees it, not only the boys who wear it. The reception of the uniform by an audience was as important, then, as the act of wearing it was for a Boy Scout.

This relationship between boys and the act of wearing the uniform can be understood as a scene-agent relationship. The uniform created a scene, and boys as agents were consistent with that scene: they were brave, adventurous, and invested in the imperial success of the nation. Any local public event at which Boy Scouts performed by wearing their uniforms became a scene of national importance in which boys were key agents. Within this relationship between the boys and the nation, boys functioned as metaphors for national power.

The first BSA uniform was adopted in 1910, including "a neckerchief, shirt, shorts or breeches, and the better-quality, stiff-brimmed Scout Hat," a uniform that Murray calls "highly practical" (143). In addition to the comfort it may have created for boys during their activities, the uniform was practical as a costume because it allowed them to perform the outdoor adventure stories integral to the Scouts. In this sense, the uniform helped to institutionalize what the Scout catalog refers to as the "psychology of Scouting." In Burkean terms, wearing the uniform—the "Act"—suggested a correlating "Agent," the type of boy who could perform an imagined rural, colonial role in the context of middle-class, urban American life.

And while it may have provided boys with a feeling of liberation in the type of play in which they were able to engage (entertaining the unrestrained physical behavior that BSA leaders and other cultural figures sought to encourage), the Boy Scout uniform also served a disciplining function. Without the uniform, the type of play the boys engaged in might have been construed as merely "savage" behavior, fitting within the established binary of the Scouting stories. With the uniform, there was no question that the boys were involved in a process of becoming civilized men, the type of men represented by the so-called great outdoorsmen who wore similar uniforms. If Scouts always wore the uniform, they would never forget that they were acting out adventure in the name of civilization and not savagery.

In his 1933 book *Lessons of a Lifetime,* Baden-Powell acknowledged the persuasive effect the uniform had had on boys, describing his plan to attract boys to the organization in its early days:

> The whole scheme was then planned on the principle of being an educative game; a recreation in which the boy would be insensibly led to educate himself. . . . [T]o call it Scouting and give him the chance of becoming an embryo Scout was [attractive]. His inherent "gang" instinct would be met by making him a member of a "Troop" and a "Patrol." Give him a uniform to wear . . . and you got him. (qtd. in Murray 8)

Baden-Powell, as well as the catalog, emphasized the uniform as an educational tool, the value of which was no doubt indirectly informed by earlier theories of education such as G. Stanley Hall's that suggested boys needed to act out the savageness that was part of their nature if they were to evolve into civilized men representative of the "master" race. Within this scene of racial evolution, the uniform functioned as an act that ensured that boys' "savageness" had a purpose in their evolution as men. This idea is conveyed in Baden-Powell's language, which suggests such a scene of natural evolution, including the phrases "embryo" and "inherent 'gang' instinct." These phrases imply a biological element in Scouting, suggesting that it is both inevitable and natural that boys participate and grow as Scouts when they don the uniform. The language of evolution creates alliances between potential consumers and the Scouting organization by creating identification based on the popularly accepted scene of scientism.

In addition to the "civilizing" function of the uniform, it was intended as a reminder that in spite of his personal fantasy of adventure, the individual boy was bound to serve the nation. This function was important because the Boy Scouts of America in many ways responded to the ambiguity and tension between the individualism of the middle-class consumer and leisure culture and the collective demands of a national identity. The connection to the nation through the uniform was reinforced by the US government with the Act of Congress of June 3, 1916 (the National Defense Act). The act prohibited unauthorized persons from wearing uniforms resembling those of the armed services but included a provision "that this was not to be construed to prevent the duly enrolled members of the Boy Scouts of America from wearing their prescribed uniform" (Murray 94). Moreover, in section VII of the congressional charter signed later that month, Congress granted the BSA "full and complete" protection of their insignia and characteristic terminology of the movement, and required US citizenship of BSA leaders and "eliminated 'alien' Scoutmasters" (Rowan 68). The government had institutionalized and legally solidified the nationalist role of the BSA by putting uniforms on the level—with its respect and responsibility—of military uniforms.

THE ROLE OF MILITARISM IN BSA RHETORIC

While the uniform symbolically suggests that the BSA was always resolutely militaristic, the role of militarism in BSA training was contested within the organization early in its history. In a 1912 speech at the National Education Association, BSA Chief Scout Executive James E. West described military training as useful only for the army, not the Boy Scouts. He argued that in Boy Scout training,

> those things which make for discipline, obedience, loyalty, courtesy, endurance, resourcefulness, initiative, alertness, moral courage, good health, knowledge of how to care for oneself, etc. should not be considered destructive military training but should be given as part of citizenship training to all boys and girls to properly prepare them primarily for their later responsibilities as home makers, wage earners, and as citizens. (qtd. in Rowan 53)

The controversy over militarism and the use of firearms in the Boy Scouts emerged publicly in 1912 when a member of the American Boy Scouts (another Scouting organization for boys) accidentally shot another boy. In his annual BSA report, West referred to that American Boy Scout as an "imitation Scout" and described the BSA as "entirely a peace movement, both in theory and practice in that it bans all military practices and that its program of activities is confined to wholesome achievements for the purpose of building character" (qtd. in Rowan 54). While the 1911 BSA handbook included a Marksmanship merit badge, the BSA awarded none of these badges that year and only twelve in 1912. When Remington Arms began offering the American Boy Scouts .22 caliber rifles in 1913, the BSA refused to adopt it (54).

This relatively pacifist stance generated criticism from some within the organization and without. The most powerful response came from Roosevelt, who argued that the organization should police national boundaries by training boys in militarism. Roosevelt refused to appear at a rally for New York City Boy Scouts of America in Madison Square Garden, writing,

> a Boy Scout who is not trained actively and affirmatively that it is his duty to bear arms for the country in time of need is at least negatively trained to be a sissy; and there cannot be

anything worse for this country than to have an organization of boys brought up to accept the mushy milk and water
which is the stock in trade of the apostles of pacifism. (qtd.
Rowan 54).

A member of the BSA executive board resigned because of a pacifist
article by Andrew Carnegie in the November 1914 issue of the
BSA magazine *Boys' Life*. Both the board member and Roosevelt
argued that the article was unpatriotic. By 1915 the BSA began
awarding more Marksmanship badges, and West softened his position on militarism, writing in his Fourth Annual Report that while
the BSA is not military in "thought, form, or spirit," it "does instill
in boys the military virtues such as honor, loyalty, obedience, and
patriotism" (qtd. in Rowan 55).

Murray's early history of the BSA omits this tension between
pacifists and militarists at an early stage in the BSA's development,
telling instead a narrative of Boy Scouts filling a universal need
for boys to become fit to represent the nation by bearing arms.
However, the conflict between pacifists and militarists points to the
important role of rhetoric in the narrative of the BSA as a national
organization. Not everyone agreed that it was best for the nation
to train boys to fight with weapons. Yet there was little possibility for the BSA to remain a pacifist organization and continue to
represent the nation because of the strength of the discourse of national masculinity at the time and the scene of embodied competition in which the BSA operated. Thus, the ambiguity over military
training became publicly resolved in favor of Roosevelt's views. The
organization's ties to Roosevelt expanded that scene to include the
United States' growing imperialism. In the public talk about boys
in the BSA by its early leaders, militarism, specifically the use of
guns, is equated with patriotism, and pacifism is aligned with an-
ti-Americanism and effeteness. Guns functioned as an agency for
patriotic service, and in the end, a boy who was successfully transitioning into American manhood would need to learn to use one.

THE BOY SCOUTS AND THE CRISIS OF CAPITALISM AT THE TURN OF THE TWENTIETH CENTURY

Murray argues that there are five areas most Boy Scout activities can relate to: the promotion of health, the learning of skills and the exploring of vocations, the stimulation of education and progress, the building of a stalwart character, and action as a participating citizen (215). In 1918, ten years after the BSA began practices in these five areas, the National Education Association's Commission of the Reorganization of Secondary Education adopted a similar list of seven cardinal principles (215), evidence of the influence of the Boy Scouts on institutionalized education.[4] The categories point to overlapping influences on the construction of American masculine national identity beyond colonial narratives, particularly the influence of the evolving capitalist marketplace, which was a key feature of the scene in which the BSA performed. Within this scene, capitalism was referred to most notably as in crisis.

To put this crisis in context, the early twentieth century was part of a history of continual crisis construction in US national identity, with crises often tied to capitalism. For example, in *National Manhood*, Dana Nelson reframes the crisis of the constitutional era "as proliferating with signs of radical democratic energies, imaginings, and practices." This framework enables her to "attend to the ways that the ideology of national manhood effectively trains, curtails, and/or shuts [those radical leanings] down" (x). In other words, the idea of national manhood was a response to perceived crisis in the cultural logic of the nation. Within Nelson's framework, the turn of the twentieth century was in fact an era of possibility, in which new forms of democracy were being imagined and racial, gender, and class practices were changing. As Roxanne Mountford has argued, the activities of the BSA functioned to curtail the possible reordering of hegemony through class, race, or gender by providing a broad organization that called on white boys to become part of the imagined fraternity of white men (44–45). By extending nationalism beyond adult males to white male children, Baden-Powell, Roosevelt, and later Boy Scout leaders ensured a new generation of masculine white men who would hold the exclusive fiction of the nation in place. The rhetoric of masculinity that the BSA performed reinforced the white capitalist patriarchal hegemony, informing people of their place in the nation.

While there were unique aspects to the turn-of-the-century constructions of national manhood that led to the formation of the Boy Scouts (such as the focus on the white male body as at once both primitive and civilized), many aspects of the crisis were new developments of old crises. The crisis at the turn of the century took several forms, though it was perceived in large part as an economic threat. As I noted in Chapter 1, capitalism's promise to men that they could become self-made was lived less frequently as large corporations became the locus of much of the economy. As wealth moved from the hands of individual middle-class business owners to increasingly large corporations, the male citizen's identity as earner was destabilized. Likewise, as the working class gained power through unions, they concentrated on working conditions that challenged the authority of middle- and upper-class men. Furthermore, when slavery ended, white male supremacy was challenged politically and in everyday life as African Americans became more publicly visible and expressed some limited power to effect political action. At the same time, the women's suffrage movement threatened to remove men as sole political decision makers. All of these economic factors were context for the scene of a crisis in manhood that needed to be overcome.

As with military training for boys, the economic element of this scene contained ambiguity. The American economy promoted individual competition, and this competition increasingly contradicted the narrative of national unity or fraternity among men. This ambiguity was not entirely new. Since the American Revolution, Nelson argues,

> [m]en whose interests had been temporarily unified in wartime were increasingly encountering fellowmen not as citizen but competitor in an unstable, rapidly changing, post-war market economy. The national need to cultivate "sameness" was threatened by the differences structured . . . by the very

market economy that supposedly ensured the nation's health. (6)

The scene of national unity was at odds with the agent—a unified nation of men—it was supposed to contain. The BSA attempted to integrate these two elements, the imagined nation of men and the competitive market identity. On the one hand, organizations like the Boy Scouts emphasize the subordination of the individual to the group. In the Boy Scouts, this subordination is taught as "cooperation." Murray explains that the Scout duty to do "Good Turn"-ing

> leads straight toward "participating citizenship.". . . He becomes a "helping part" almost unconsciously and quite painlessly. . . . Such habits of cooperation probably are essential, if one is to fit smoothly and helpfully into the present-day scheme of life. Research done at Columbia in the past few years has reported that Scouts cooperate conspicuously better than non-Scouts. (228)

And yet fitting "smoothly and helpfully," in the context of the early-twentieth-century nation, meant helping the economy to function.

So, paradoxically, while boys learned a rhetoric of independent strength and self-control, they were also placed in a position of great dependence because of the BSA's emphasis on the group. The group emphasis was echoed throughout white male American life. As evidence for this emphasis, Rotundo quotes an excerpt from Oliver Wendell Holmes Jr.'s 1895 speech, "The Soldier's Faith":

> The faith is true and adorable which leads a soldier to throw away his life in obedience to a blindly accepted duty, in a cause which he little understands, in a plan of campaign of which he has no notion, under tactics of which he does not see the use. (237)

Again, the emphasis on the group, when paired uncomfortably with the rhetoric of the individual, was not peculiar to the turn of the twentieth century, but rather was a feature of American capitalism generally. Since the beginning of the United States, white manhood, as part of capitalism's promise, has appealed to a group through the idea of a nationally shared "nature." Dana Nelson writes that "[f]ormer colonials of European descent, increasingly competitors in the market and political economies, could share collectively the exclusive property of 'whiteness'—a category that subordinated European national and colonial/state identifications as it 'democratically' wedded men to the new United States" (7). The imagined unity of national manhood rhetoric disguised the competitive difference that the market economy created. It also gave men a new kind of exclusive collective property, "whiteness," creating a new American identity after the American Revolution.

While the group identity of boys as agents may have at times had an ambiguous relationship to the scene of individual competition, the BSA also took up the cause of capitalism by focusing on how a Scout should handle his money, as well as encouraging competition and emphasizing private property. The ninth part of the Scout Law states that "A Scout is Thrifty." In the remaining text of the law, we can see the focus on the individual within the market economy, which sharply contrasts to the focus on subordination to the group present in the other laws (e.g., Law 7: "A Scout is Obedient," Law 2: "A Scout is Loyal," and Law 3: A Scout is Helpful."):

> 9. A SCOUT IS THRIFTY. He does not wantonly destroy property. He works faithfully, wastes nothing, and makes the best use of his opportunities. He saves his money so that he may pay his own way, be generous to those in need, and helpful to worthy objects. He may work for pay but must not receive tips for courtesies or good turns. (qtd. in Murray 63)

The emphasis on capitalism in this version of the law is evident when it is compared with the original British version, which contrasts to the American law's emphasis on private property, unrelenting work, individual opportunity, financial self-sufficiency, and the worth of those whom the Boy Scout might help:

> 9. A SCOUT IS THRIFTY, that is he saves every penny he can, and puts it into the bank, so that he may have money to keep himself when out of work, and thus not make himself a

burden to the others; or that he may have money to give away to others when they need it. (qtd. in Murray 63)

In fact, the British law suggests that the Boy Scout (and his needy acquaintances) might very well be out of work one day, an idea that is impossible within the scene of the BSA, with its American promise of success as a reward for hard work. While the British and the American Scouts shared an investment in whiteness, the American organization incorporated this whiteness into the market economy and the American values of private property and individual success.

It is important to note the historical intersection between private property and whiteness in the United States. Legal scholar Cheryl Harris has demonstrated that whiteness itself has historically functioned as property through US legal systems. This legal support "converted an aspect of identity into an external object of property, moving whiteness from privileged identity to a vested interest" (1725). By directly and indirectly invoking whiteness throughout its early discourse, the BSA participated in a broad cultural process of reifying a racial concept that was simultaneously gaining legal existence. So because of several influences, race was a fixture of the scene that the BSA imagined collectively.

Capitalism was also a fixture of that scene, and the BSA buoyed the discourse of white masculinity by encouraging the individual competition that was compatible with the capitalist market through which white men gained power. In other words, members were guided to act consistently with that scene. In competitions involving skills such as knot tying, applying roller bandages and tent pitching, the BSA encouraged boys to compete against themselves and other members. "Here," Murray writes, "the Scout has faced the job of squaring his own results with high standards of skill and excellence" (231). Such competition would prepare men ideologically to participate as individuals in the relentless competition of the market. Rotundo notes that by the turn of the twentieth century, men were increasingly describing their lives, work in particular, in the language of competition. He quotes a Denver lawyer at the end of the nineteenth century as saying, "Here is a vast field for workers and vast amounts of money to be gotten, if I am only equal to the contest I shall win, if weak then some other and stronger one will carry off the spoils" (244). But, Rotundo argues, competition worked its way beyond economic and political spheres into solitary life activities such as Sunday school classes, where teachers offered prizes to the best students "in the hope of hastening salvation of souls and increasing student interest at the same time" (245). In guarding the nation's economy, boys in organizations like the BSA were encouraged to take up the discourse of competition with fervor.

Yet in this element of BSA motives there was ambiguity as well. For example, in March 1912, Baden-Powell of the British Boy Scouts came to the United States for a lecture tour on which he was accompanied by James West from the BSA. As Baden-Powell and West addressed an audience in Portland, Oregon, they were "hooted off the stage . . . by International Workers of the World [IWW] members incensed by what they perceived to be [Baden-Powell's] antiunion comments in the first printing of the Handbook" (Rowan 48). IWW members also objected to the BSA's practice of using Boy Scouts as "uniformed strike-breakers" (48). Adding to union antipathy was the fact that Boy Scouts of America was predominantly middle class according to its own demographic profiles (Rowan 48). So while the scene of capitalist competition worked for many audiences, it did not explain the motives of all male audiences.

CONCLUSION

The Boy Scouts of America functioned as a site that both reflected and produced the United States' cultural contradictions, helping to form the scene of American masculinity and to constitute hegemonic American male identity. But, as Charland argues, "[s]uccessful new constitutive rhetorics offer new subject positions that resolve, or at least contain, experienced contradictions. They serve to overcome or define away the recalcitrance the world presents by providing the subject with new perspectives and motives" (142). The rhetorical practices of the early BSA were successfully constitutive to the extent that they proffered to American boys an identity that resolved the contradiction between allegiance to the nation, with its promises of international superiority and domestic capitalist possibility, and the economic disappointments of lived American capitalism.

The language practices of the BSA mediated lived experience for many boys in the United States by producing a discourse of American identity tied to whiteness, capitalist market participation, and colonialist national logic. The BSA's ideal American boy lived inside the rhetoric that constructed him (Stein 173). The organization's textual and visual discourse about the Boy Scout experience—the "Unknown Scout" origin myth, the oath, the congressional charter, the uniform, debates in Scouting magazines about the role of weapons training, and the earliest published history of the organization written by a Scout leader—framed these boys' experiences of hope personally, narrating boys into "subjects-as-agents" oriented toward particular future acts (Charland 143) and presenting hope for a future of fulfillment and a definition of that fulfillment that centered on national participation. For females and those males outside of the BSA's target audience (gay boys and those whose bodies couldn't be circumscribed by BSA discourse, for example), the BSA's scene of transformation from boyhood to manhood did not offer any possible identification. At the same time, by formally welcoming boys of color (even though the organization was not always racially open in practice and its discourse supported white hegemony), the BSA implied that everyone male could participate in the process of becoming American men that the organization promoted. As discussed, the organization's capitalist values and colonial stories also centralized whiteness as characteristic of members and placed the organization at rhetorical odds with racial integration. One could argue, in fact, that whiteness was an agency of masculinity. Unlike the audible tension surrounding the issues of militarizing the Boy Scouts by training boys to use weapons and using boys as strikebreakers, the contradiction between this idea of race and the organization's openness to boys of color was obscured by the BSA's language of character building, enabling the scene of hegemonic masculinity to abide as a popular guide for boys and parents, potential agents.

3

Constituting American Fraternity Members through the Rhetoric of Becoming

IF BOYS IN THE UNITED STATES MISS the opportunity for masculinity training at a young age through the Boy Scouts of America, another possibility awaits many of those who attend universities on their way to participating in the middle and upper classes. The Greek fraternity was a twentieth-century fixture at colleges and universities across the country, with a history slightly longer than that of the BSA. And while fraternities and fraternity members have sometimes been objects of public criticism in the second half of the twentieth century as well as today for the ways they have enacted masculinity, these organizations have nonetheless been a key source of masculinity construction, creating a discourse about the transition from boyhood into hegemonic manhood. To read fraternities through Burke is to uncover some of the motives for participation in this type of organization and to analyze how, despite regular controversies, these relatively old (at least in US terms) organizations have prevailed. Such a reading exploits the usefulness of Burke's concept of constitutive rhetoric, stretching the term beyond the national constitutions that were Burke's focus.

Young American males entering college at the traditional age of eighteen face transitions both material and imagined, as they often relocate geographically and economically, but their age is something of an undefined stage of manhood in popular culture. College-age males no longer are seen as boys, as are most members of the BSA, yet they are not viewed as fully developed men either. Organizations for college males are unique, therefore, in their attempt to define this stage for groups of middle-class males. Traditionally, college-bound males in the United States leave home and live independent of their nuclear families for the first time, surrounded by new opportunities for identifying apart from their families and former peers. In a new place and space, they enter social and institutional settings that interpellate them anew. As with the other organizations explored in this study, this transition itself has gained its social meaning through the way it has been written and talked about rather than through any intrinsic qualities, and Burke's dramatistic model gives us a way to understand the motives behind the performances of masculinity that have been engendered by the organizations' discursive sense-making in such an imaginary space.

Like the BSA, mainstream white college fraternities define male members as men-in-the-making through a rhetoric of becoming that contains class and race boundaries along with its more obvious gender constraints. As with the Boy Scouts, college fraternities have historically offered young males a means to imagine themselves as economic beings by adopting an identity in relation to the marketplace. Also like the boys in the BSA, males in most fraternities historically have been pushed to perform whiteness, though as in the BSA, these performances are complicated by concomitant narratives of openness to racial diversity. However, fraternities are unlike the BSA because of their more explicit focus on social class distinction intertwined with race. This chapter focuses on one fraternity chapter, Sigma Chi at Columbia University, whose documents reveal this focus through terms that emerge repeatedly, sometimes encoded as *democracy, values,* and *character.*

These terms are important because they demonstrate that the rhetorical project of building white masculine identity is typically a project of building national identity. As fraternities develop a rhetoric of transitioning into manhood or "becoming," they are defining what it means to be American. Their rhetoric of becoming consists of two layers. First, Greek social organizations offer a rhetorical apparatus that constitutes or calls into being an organization's members as subjects or agents. Through this process, individual males are guided to identify as a particular type of American male—in this case, one of a potential elite. The second layer of rhetoric constructs becoming itself—that is, it constructs the possibility or scene in which young adult males are at a crossroads, a point of transition they must pass through to become men. By focusing on Sigma Chi at Columbia during the 1960s as emblematic, I demonstrate how this context-bound process works.

I begin with the Burkean and post-Burkean concept of constitutive rhetoric because of the special role of Sigma Chi's old foundational documents in creating more recent identity for members. Theories of constitutive rhetoric have focused on foundational national documents as the most potent frameworks for collective identification. Kenneth Burke launched this focus in *A Grammar of Motives* by arguing that a constitution is the most appropriate representative anecdote for analyzing identification because it points to how motives converge to construct the *agent*, the first of his dramatistic terms, which he introduces in *A Grammar of Motives'* final chapter, "The Dialectic of Constitutions" (323). For Burke, constitutions create the possibilities for a society's view of who its members are and how they view outsiders: "Indeed, in actual point of fact," he writes, "a Constitution is addressed by the first person to the second. In propounding a Constitution, 'I' or 'we' say what 'you' may or should and may not or should not do" (360). He places the subjects of constitutions within a conflictual scene, writing that "[c]onstitutions are agonistic instruments. They involve an enemy, implicitly or explicitly" (357). In describing how constitutions construct agents who speak to one another and to outsiders, Burke puts into rhetorical terms what theorists of nationalism have subsequently described as a central component of nationalism, the boundary between "we" and "them" that emerges from a national community's shared sense of history, ethnicity, or language, among other factors (Duara 168; Smith, "Origins" 124–26; B. Anderson 7).

Audiences identify themselves into being, but foundational documents create the call to do so and thus shape the way audiences identify. Maurice Charland extended Burke's line of analysis in his article "Constitutive Rhetoric: The Case of the *Peuple Québécois*" by arguing that audiences of constitutive rhetoric are interpellated or hailed as subjects in the Althusserian sense (138). Charland argues that constitutive rhetoric creates the possibilities for structuring the way that audiences identify. In such a framework, audiences enter the discourse as part of a collective, transcendent subject with the illusion of freedom but bound by the narrative of the constitutive text (140–41). This illusion of freedom and its concomitant boundaries applies to Sigma Chi.

At this point, I reiterate my argument that the constitution of national identity occurs meaningfully in local organizations with national affiliation, and often through seemingly quotidian statements and actions. As Drew Loewe has pointed out in his analysis of constitutive rhetoric, the critical considerations that Burke applies to constitutions also apply to a range of symbolic action. I offer college fraternities' foundational documents as an example of symbolic action that falls in this range by using a constitutive rhetoric of becoming. In presenting this rhetoric of becoming, college fraternities' seminal documents constitute a male agent who is the source of present and future acts, just as Burke's US Constitution creates such a subject. In particular, fraternities' handbooks do the work of constituting identity along gender, class, and race-bound parameters, often using vague but powerful "god terms," as Burke would say. Through these articulations, young fraternity members can identify with the image of a fraternity member that the documents make available.

Sigma Chi fraternity, a male-only fraternity founded in 1855, has reflected many American college fraternities during its history, beginning as a literary society at Miami University of Ohio and spreading nationally as other campuses opened affiliated chapters, including the one at Columbia University. It possesses a unique origin myth and organizational creed, both published in its handbook and both of which affected members many decades later.

Like other fraternities at Columbia, Sigma Chi responded to declining campus interest in fraternities during the 1960s and 1970s. For Sigma Chi, this decline began in the 1950s, when the issue of racial exclusion became prominent (Begenau; Grabenstein; Minov). It continued into the 1980s, when the Columbia University chapter faced the possibility of being forced to admit women, though that possibility did not materialize. During this era of an uncertain future, Sigma Chi members publicly expressed rationales for the organization's existence in the campus newspaper and in the *New York Times*, responding to critical questions from outsiders about the organization's function. Therefore, one could say that at that point, the scene was, in fact, agonistic.

BACKGROUND AND CONTEXT

Fraternities have not been explored in great depth by academics. In 2009, Nicholas L. Syrett provided the first chronology and historical analysis of fraternities in the United States, addressing class, race, and sexuality as elements of the masculinity these organizations construct. Fraternities were popular at Columbia[1] until the early 1960s, when their popularity dropped as student politics on campus moved left. In 1964, in response to a Supreme Court case, Columbia (along with other universities nationally) forced its fraternities to remove any bias clauses from their charters and to end practices that discriminated against pledges based on race. While most fraternities at Columbia appear to have done this fairly quietly and quickly, Sigma Chi held out changing its charter until the last possible day because its national (parent) organization refused to sign the "Declaration of Nondiscriminatory Practices" that Columbia required ("Non-Bias Oath"). A 1971 article in the *Columbia Spectator* points out that at the last minute the fraternity complied with Columbia's policy, and as a result the national organization revoked its charter (Gura). As a result, the Columbia chapter was left an orphan entity with no national affiliation. The Columbia chapter of Sigma Chi remained at Columbia, renamed Nu Sigma Chi, and began admitting members regardless of race or religion. Within a few years, however, fraternity membership had declined at Columbia significantly (Gura). According to a 1967 article in the student paper, *Columbia Spectator*, in 1922, 51 percent of Columbia students were in fraternities, but by 1967, only 25 percent were ("Fraternities' Future"). By 1976, only 5–10 percent of Columbia's students were in a fraternity (K. Hall), and this decline would last until the 1980s, always attended by public protests against fraternities from nonmembers.

These acute and chronic membership crises gave rise to public statements from members of Sigma Chi and its opponents about the nature and purpose of fraternities. During the decline of the 1960s and 1970s, a corresponding increase in members' public statements in student publications argued for the good of fraternity membership and justified the organizations' existence at Columbia. Columbia's archives demonstrate arguments both for and against the existence of fraternities on Columbia's campus, with students on both sides arguing at length in the student paper and in the alumni magazine.

While the midcentury debate over racial bias in fraternities came to a conclusion, the uneasiness over fraternities at Columbia continued. Protests of fraternity membership at Columbia arose in the 1980s, and Sigma Chi members' public statements continued to reflect the organization's internal discourse. In the mid-1980s, fraternities at Columbia once again faced a threat to membership when a vocal group of students argued that all fraternities on the campus should become coed. At that point, there were twelve all-male fraternities, six coed fraternities, and three all-female sororities (Kaufman). The argument that all fraternities should become coeducational was made most often by a group called Students for a Reformed Fraternity System (SFRFS) but was also engaged by students from Barnard College (Meier, "Coed Fraternity") and became a campaign platform for candidates in student council elections that year (Meier, "Frat Forum"). The debate erupted into a shouting match during at least one public meeting on the topic (Meier, "Coed Fraternity"). The leader of SFRFS, University Senator Tom Kamber, implied that SFRFS members received death threats (Gillette). According to an SFRFS member quoted in the *Columbia Daily Spectator*, the only argument in favor of fraternities remaining all male was that it allows members to walk around freely in their underwear (Meier, "Frat Forum"). The argument against fraternities remaining all-male, according to the same article, was that fraternity members have committed sexual abuse and harassment.

The agonistic environment of public statements about membership had reached new heights.

The public statements that fraternity members made about their organization in response to this more recent crisis reflect the internal discourse of the organization that revealed itself during the 1960s and 1970s. We can see the importance of Sigma Chi's foundational documents to members by the way they were used as a means of explaining the fraternity members' actions in one debate moderated by Columbia College Dean Robert Pollack in April 1988. In this debate, a Sigma Chi member argued that while date rape and sexual harassment were problems, they came from universities generally and not single-sex organizations (Meier, "Frat Forum"). "There's nothing in our charter that says, 'Let's go men,' at the exclusion of women," the member argued. Another fraternity member drew from the historical legacy of all-male fraternities to justify their existence, arguing that the fact that the system had been around for 200 years was evidence of how well it worked (Meier, "Frat Forum"). On another occasion, a member echoed this claim to the deep history of Greek organizations in the United States by claiming that fraternities remaining all-male "has nothing to do with sexism; it has to do with tradition" (Lee).

My point in mentioning these more recent examples before examining earlier statements is to demonstrate the degree to which the ideology of the founding documents had been absorbed by members at that point, to the extent of sounding absurd. But this stage of entrenched identification evolved from decades of testing the power of Sigma Chi's constitutive rhetoric to shape identity in moments of conflict. And the power seems to have been diminishing, as some of the strongest arguments against same-sex fraternities came from former members. While one fraternity member argued that any sexual abusers in fraternities are "bad apples," a former member (who did not find the SFRFS to be persuasive, because of their lack of insider knowledge about fraternities) explained how fraternities' all-male environment works to hide and perpetuate sexism and sexual harassment: "When there is opposition, because of a rape or something, fraternities have an automatic system that protects itself. Because they're so secretive, it's hard to single out incidents of rape. Women who go to their parties and are raped are made to think 'It's my fault.' It becomes an individual against 40 guys" (Meier, "Frat Forum"). The debate over requiring fraternities to accept women escalated over the course of the academic year, with SFRFS members holding a silent vigil outside a fraternity and the activists claiming that Sigma Chi fraternity members threw beer and spat on them, calling them "homos" and "bitches" (Meier and Shultz).

The protracted crisis of Sigma Chi losing its national charter in the early 1960s and the debate in the mid-1980s demonstrate that the scene in which Sigma Chi's foundational documents exist has changed over the course of the fraternity's existence, although the documents have remained the same and have continued to provide key terms such as *tradition* that serve to justify the organization's existence. While the Sigma Chi handbook and other documents once supported an organization of white, Christian men of means, after the mid-1960s, in a nation and on a campus less able to accept overt racial segregation, fraternity members defended their identification with the organization as a group of men chosen according to vague traits such as their commitment to "tradition," "brotherhood," "values," and "democracy." Although the organization sustained membership levels that kept the organization functional at Columbia, the ambiguity between the scene and its acts and agents seems to have grown.

Records show that while students arguing against fraternities have decried the organizations in somewhat specific terms such as racial discrimination, sexual harassment, and assault, fraternity members have framed their arguments in vaguer, indefinable, yet unquestionable terms, what Burke calls "god terms" (Burke, *Rhetoric* 299–301), in actions that correspond with a scene of emerging manhood. While fraternity membership is by definition exclusive and provides access to an alumni network of former members who can help current members beyond the boundary of college life as they make their way socially and economically, members talk publicly about their membership using these god terms that cloud the insider element and naturalize fraternity membership.

SIGMA CHI AS A SPACE OF TRANSITION

In its "talk about" membership, to recall Burke's phrase, Sigma Chi constructs members as occupying a transformational and transitional space, reifying the idea that through the act of membership during college, boys will be transformed into men. We see this construction in the early pages of Sigma Chi's manual, *The Norman Shield*, which notes that "Sigma Chi is not a destination, but a journey; a quest to develop throughout life as a citizen, a man, and a brother" (Church 8). In this and similar statements, the manual creates a common tie between members within a chapter at a given campus and between members nationally, hailing them as American men who belong in a specific setting—who exist as men within the fraternity and at the same time within the nation. The statement might raise the question for some readers: can this transition happen outside of a fraternity?

The manual suggests that the answer is "no" as it continues its claim: "The advantage of a fraternity over many other groups of individuals is that it more closely approaches the ideal background for fraternal feeling" (Church 16). With this statement, the manual brings into existence this ideal background, suggesting that an imperfect background can fail to create fraternal feeling, or perhaps that an imperfect background creates the wrong kind of fraternal feeling. Why this is so is not explained and does not need to be, because *ideal* and *fraternal* serve as god terms, repeated words or phrases indicating values that are above question. The vagueness of the manual's assertion that the fraternity "more closely approaches" the right means to manhood is irrelevant because the other elements of identification are so strong: appeals to tradition, superiority, and belonging. Readers understand that the comparison is to those who attend college outside of membership.

The words *brothers* and *brotherhood* also emphasize the idea that Sigma Chi offers a natural relationship that stands without questioning. As with *ideal background*, the manual does not articulate exactly what *brotherhood* is; it too is a god term. By positioning fraternity members as brothers, the manual constitutes members as part of a family, defined through their relationship to other family members. As brothers within a family (as opposed to full citizens within a nation, for example), fraternity members are dependent, neither able to act independently nor bearing responsibility for their actions entirely alone.

The family connection is further emphasized as an enduring connection through other god terms. To *brotherhood* the manual adds *commitment* and *noble values* in describing the role of the ritual in ensuring that these ideas obtain:

> If strong and enduring brotherhood among men who share commitment to noble values is the purpose of Sigma Chi, then the Ritual must serve as a guide in fulfilling that purpose. . . . The Ritual is kept secret from non-members for several reasons. Secrecy creates a feeling of uniqueness and therefore helps to strengthen the bonds that initiated brothers share. More importantly, the secrecy provides for a learning process for potential members, so that they can learn more about what Sigma Chi stands for before committing themselves to its ideals. And it is that commitment of our brothers that makes initiation into Sigma Chi a unique honor—and responsibility. (Church 27)

Throughout the manual, terms such as *brotherhood, commitment,* and *ideals* tap into cultural commonplaces that lack a precise meaning but that carry great symbolic weight. Because they are vague, they are also impossible to oppose directly, and for members and potential members, they are likely to have positive meanings. These terms encourage identification with concepts that connote national belonging.

These vague terms work for many members because they are cloaked in the performance of rituals. In *Attitudes toward History,* Burke describes the ritual of becoming through which organizations like Sigma Chi involve their young male members. "Identity," Burke writes, "involves 'change of identity' insofar as any given structure of society calls forth conflicts among our corporate we's. From this necessity you get . . . the various ritualizations of rebirth" (268–69). In other words, as a person experiences an incongruity between identification with an old group and identification with a new group, or what Burke terms *corporate identity,* he must change his identity to accommodate his new group membership. For example, a couple who has their first child might begin to identify less with their childless peers and more with other couples who have young children. Yet, Burke points out, a person's identity is additive rather than formed from complete revolutions; "since the twice born begins as one man and becomes another, he is at once a continuum and a duality" (269). In this way, Sigma Chi offers a new vision of family, transferring dependence on a boy's actual parents to dependence on fellow fraternity members whom he thinks of as "brothers." This new identification encourages members to act and explain their actions as part of a new collective family.

The organization's documents demonstrate that members understand their project as additive in this way. According to Sigma Chi's current alumni webpage and several local chapter webpages, the fraternity intercedes in the "continuum of character development that assists young men to develop the qualities of their character." Sigma Chi replicates the common idea that character comes from family initially and is a reflection of inherent qualities that are nurtured in a particular way. The scene is the family and the community as a collection of families, the agent is a brother, and the agency is fraternity membership and rituals.

Of course, unlike most families, the Sigma Chi fraternity is exclusive, choosing its members based on their presentation. Not everyone can belong. But at the same time, the language in the manual implies that Sigma Chi membership is natural, enduring, and a defining feature of mainstream society. In using the word *brother,* the handbook naturalizes and legitimizes the relationship between members. It encourages pledges to identify with a collective that is natural yet exclusive. It is, in a sense, like belonging to a highly successful and influential family, one that would be likely to produce successful male heirs.

The relevance of the familial identity that contributes to Sigma Chi's rhetoric of becoming is apparent when one examines its influence on statements in the Columbia alumni newsletter by a Columbia fraternity member in 1962, the year that Sigma Chi faced its first membership crisis, and as the issue of racial discrimination in Sigma Chi's national charter prompted public discussion about the value of fraternities at Columbia. The member argued that young men need small-scale exchanges among themselves to build "brains and character," adding that fraternities "provide a perfect-sized unit in which to grow intellectually and emotionally" (Kelso 18). He explained that fraternities give young males their "first taste of adult responsibilities." Fraternity members develop "pride, good sense, and maturity" in running their houses (Kelso 20). Perhaps most telling of his identification with the manual, the member argued that fraternities promote the growth of "brotherhood and idealism." His statement, like the manual, leaves these terms undefined.

Because fraternity "brotherhood" lacks the enduring biological and/or legal connection that defines the ideal nuclear family, this connection is produced and consumed through a ritual, much as a marriage between two partners is legitimized as a relationship through a ritual. The role of "the Ritual" (always capitalized in *The Norman Shield*) in Sigma Chi members' identity formation is expressed in the following explanation in the handbook:

> Only careful practice of the Ritual's ceremony and procedure will ensure that all Sigma Chis share a common experience. Otherwise, we risk not only losing identity as an organization but also weakening the bonds that extend from chapter to chapter and generation to generation. (Church 27)

In this description of the ritual, identity is not a personal quality held by individuals but rather something that is experienced when members act as a group through a formal, prescribed set of behaviors that the manual does not describe. The ritual transforms its participants. Fraternity identity, according to the manual, occurs only when members perform exact repetition of the ritual. Members transform as a result of participating in the ritual, but individual members have no effect on the ritual; that is, the ritual itself does not change in response to new members, new ideas, or new contexts. As it is presented in the manual, the ritual ensures that member identity is constant, does not evolve or change, and must be carefully maintained across geography and time. As the handbook continues, "Because of [the] great environmental differences among our undergraduate institutions, the Ritual is our only reliable and lasting source of common ground" (Church 27). Exactly how the ritual ensures common ground and why it is reliable is not explained; the common ground that members enact is the performance of the ritual itself.

Burke's treatment of ritual in *Attitudes toward History* helps to explain the persuasive importance of ritual for Sigma Chi. While the idea that ritual helps to maintain stability in communities[2] has been widely studied, Burke argues that ritual also persuades participants to believe in its power (Gibson). For Burke, participants are actively involved in the persuasive effect that a ritual has on them. Although details about the Sigma Chi ritual are not easily available to nonmembers and so we cannot know what kinds of symbolism or intonation, for example, they might invoke, we can see the way *The Norman Shield* presents the ritual to members—in other words, we can see some of the "talk about" the ritual. By capitalizing "Ritual" and by speaking of it in vague terms—in fact, by making the contents of the ritual a secret to be shared in person between members—the writers of the handbook and those who use the handbook to understand the organization ritualize the ritual itself. Members themselves, having participated in the ritual, are led to understand that they have created—and been created by—a brotherhood bond that separates them from nonmembers.

BROTHERHOOD IDENTIFICATION AND CLASS

In transforming into the men that Sigma Chi encourages members to imagine themselves becoming, young men must shift from one identity to another. Burke describes changes in identity as an act of "seeing around a corner." That is, when one moves from an old to a new identity, he is seeing from two angles at once. Burke writes,

> From this shift of co-ordinates . . . [a person] derives his "perspective." In a sense, all perspectives are "seeing from two angles at once"\' (quite as the stereopticon camera gives the

sense of depth by putting two different focuses upon a subject and remerging them, whereas the one-eyed camera sees flat). The change gives one a sense of direction; hence he "prophesies." (*Attitudes* 270)

Seeing from two perspectives, that from which an individual used to identify and that from which he now identifies, allows him to see more deeply into matters connected to his identities, past and present. When members of the Sigma Chi fraternity read the handbook, join the organization, and participate in its rituals—both formal organization rituals and informal rituals such as behaving according to the guidelines in the handbook—they are encouraged to understand their class positions from a new angle and with more depth than they did before they joined. For those who come from middle-class backgrounds, the handbook's guidance on manners, for example, suggests to them that they must behave in particular ways to gain access to the most "polite" spaces of society and that these polite spaces matter for their development into men. From this new identity perspective, young men can look back on their former lives with the understanding that they must change in order to be a full member. They can also understand that such manners are part of the power the organization develops in them. Yet Burke also argues that forgetting is important to identification, even as he writes that a change in identity brings about a dual identity (271) and dual vision. Even as fraternity members are confronted with the performance of identity they must maintain through adhering to manners, they are encouraged to forget their identities as middle class through the very performance of those manners.

Following the description of ritual, the manual's focus on manners suggests that class—specifically the performance of class—is an important component of fraternity membership. Apparently Sigma Chi admits members who the organization cannot assume have already integrated into their identities American upper-class markers such as making appropriate fork choices, proper bodily grooming, and knowing how to graciously escort a "lady." Yet the fraternity places great value on these traditional rituals. The manual gives considerable space to describing how to match sock color to pant color, how to tie a tie, how to walk beside a lady, and how to butter bread, among other instructions. For example, the handbook advises that men should always rise when a "lady" or "older gentleman" enters a room (Church 30). Rather than being included in an appendix or other secondary spot within the text, this advice appears between sections on the ritual and the history of fraternities. That this information has a prominent place in the book—that it is included at all—is evidence that this organization functions in part as a means for members to gain access to a culture of manners. The manners guidelines themselves are not remarkable; what is remarkable is that the organization is choosing members who it assumes may not have learned them during their upbringing. In this way, it aims at transformation through performance and costume designed to make upper-class men out of those from middle-class families. The performance is heavily gendered, as traditional manners are, and so encourages a manly gender identification that coincides with class distinction.

ORIGIN MYTH

Sigma Chi, like the other organizations for young males I address, explains its history by way of an origin story told in the handbook, and this origin story helps shape the way that members identify with the organization; in other words, it is a key part of the scene in which members are agents. Sigma Chi's origin story begins in 1854, before the fraternity formed, and focuses on a rift that year between members of another fraternity, Miami University's Delta Kappa Epsilon (DKE). DKE members disagreed about supporting a fellow member who was running for the office of poet in Miami University's literary society (Church). According to the story in the Sigma Chi handbook, six DKE members believed that all members of their fraternity should support the candidate as a fellow fraternity member, and six others believed they should support whichever candidate they felt was the most qualified for the role of poet, regardless of whether he was a DKE member or not. The handbook's account of the rift is detailed, and the details are framed as a ratio between an act—whether merit or loyalty should have warranted fraternity members' votes—and a purpose—whether fraternity members should support one another in all circumstances or should abide by a sense of merit that extended beyond the fraternity. The first sentence of the section "The Founding of Sigma Chi" makes this ratio clear, explaining that "[f]ittingly, Sigma Chi was born out of a matter of principle" (Church). The text concludes that a "commitment to justice" led to six members of the small DKE fraternity leaving to form their own fraternity, Sigma Chi.

Unlike the Boy Scouts of America, whose history in fact includes disagreements and rivalries between founders but whose origin myth presents a mysterious and apparently fabricated story of the Unknown Scout's cooperation and servitude, Sigma Chi's origin story valorizes the role of disagreement and antagonism in support of principles. A prominent element of Sigma Chi's origin story is the focus on Benjamin Piatt Runkle, one of the members of DKE who, once expelled from that fraternity because of his belief in merit rather than loyalty, went on to form Sigma Chi along with his five sympathizers. According to the story, Runkle and the other five believers in merit called a dinner meeting with the six DKE supporters of loyalty in order to reconcile their differences. The DKE loyalists did not show up for the dinner, except for one member who appeared with a DKE alumnus, who proclaimed that the six recalcitrant meritocrats must be expelled from the fraternity. In response, Runkle tore off his DKE badge and threw it on the dinner table, shouting, "I didn't join this fraternity to be anyone's tool. And that, sir, is my answer!" (Church). With this statement, the story recounts, Runkle stalked out of the room, followed by his five like-minded "brothers." The six were expelled from DKE and went on to form Sigma Chi fraternity.

Runkle is honored in *The Norman Shield* for being fearless and "courageous in spirit and idealism" in a biography section on the founders of Sigma Chi subtitled "Who they are, and why we honor their names." In enumerating Runkle's achievements, the handbook describes his fascination with the Roman emperor Constantine[3] as a heroic figure whose "vision on the night before the battle for Rome" inspired Runkle's idea for the White Cross, the Sigma

Chi insignia (Church). It also describes as an example of Runkle's courage and idealism his temporary suspension from Ohio University for "fighting in chapel with a member of Beta Theta Pi who had publicly sneered at his [Sigma Chi] badge." In the origin story and subsequent honoring of Runkle, the handbook paints the scene of Sigma Chi's founding as one of righting values that had gone askew. In this context, Runkle and his five sympathizers performed an act that was congruent with the purpose (justice based on merit) that the origin story constructs. Framed in this context, Runkle's rebelliousness and aggression is a fitting response to injustice, and his acts righted the wrong that had been committed by the other DKE members when they insisted on loyalty above merit-based action.

The dramatistic purpose-act ratio set up in this story framed the fraternity more generally for members of subsequent generations. Sigma Chi is, by extension, a scene of principles and justice, a space that has been fought for and won through a revolution. The origin story contains parallels with the American Revolution as an account of unfair demands for loyalty being made on those who demanded that merit be rewarded. Sigma Chi, then, is a scene of firmly held principles that echo the deepest-held principles of American national identity. The act of standing up for independence and individual merit is a familiar one in US national mythology, and the Sigma Chi origin story taps into this element of national identity in constituting its members as a group. With the role of this myth in mind, it is easy to see how Columbia's Sigma Chi members could adhere so stubbornly to their organization's bias clause more than 100 years later.

Like the idea of loyalty, the role of merit in the origin story echoes the pre-Revolution idea of the Protestant work ethic that has helped define the United States as a meritocracy. This element of the myth also helps to explain values of the organization described earlier, suggesting that there is a fundamental rift between those who succeed based on merit and those who operate based on an unfounded loyalty that leads fellow members to succeed despite their qualifications. The myth also indirectly supports the racially exclusive membership policies that came to the forefront in debates at Columbia over fraternity membership in the 1960s. The connection between the myth's idea of merit and exclusivity seems to surface when a member justifies fraternity bias clauses: "One would think that 'discrimination' had lost its meaning of making nice judgments and that 'democracy' was synonymous with *potpourri*," he writes (qtd. in Kelso 22). The member implies that fraternities are justified in excluding members of color because they would not live up to the standards of being principled and having merit. With the scene set by the origin myth in the handbook, even the act of racial discrimination could be justified because it was contained within that scene.

SIGMA CHI AS CONSTITUTING IDENTITY

Like many other organizations for young males, fraternities frame and limit members' possible interpretations of their experiences, binding them in a language of transformation into men of strong character who possess the right values. Among the values repeated in the handbook is democracy. However, unlike the BSA, which claims to be open to all boys regardless of race, class, or religion, Sigma Chi emphasizes its exclusivity as an organization for exceptional young men at the same time it refers to democracy as a key value. In its use of the word *democracy,* the handbook implies that the organization is quintessentially American. This use of the term *democracy* is drawn on by the fraternity member from 1962 whom I cited in the preceding paragraph. He framed his defense of fraternities at Columbia by arguing that the small environment of fraternities permits conversations about "the nature of God or the future of communism, true democracy in running the affairs of the house." ("Fraternities at Columbia"). This statement contains a subtle implication that outside of the fraternity, Columbia is a less democratic and deliberative space and that the fraternity environment breeds insight that leads to better democracy. He reconciles what seems like a conflict between democracy and the organization's exclusivity by arguing that democracy allows for bias, using the language cited in part earlier:

Perhaps the most frequent charge against fraternities is that they are "biased" in their selection of members. This assertion has been material for numerous sensational magazine and newspaper articles in recent years. One would think that "discrimination" had lost its meaning of making nice judgments and that "democracy" was synonymous with *potpourri*. Nevertheless, it is necessary to admit that several national fraternities (three of them represented at Columbia) still do have "bias clauses." In defense, it is equally necessary to say that the Columbia chapters have been in the forefront of those seeking to eliminate such clauses. Since 1950, the College's Pamphratria [Columbia's interfraternity council] has opposed them. (Kelso 22)

In his claims, the member justifies the exclusive, even racially discriminatory practices of fraternities by placing them within the parameters of American democracy, at the same time that he appears to support eliminating bias clauses among Columbia's fraternities. His words contain a sense of potential ambiguity between his identity as a fraternity member and his identity as a Columbia College student.

Sigma Chi's manual is constitutive as a document that shapes young men's identities by advising them on how they should act because they are a select group of American males of high character in the process of becoming exceptional men. Burke explains that "what a Constitution would do primarily is to *substantiate an ought* (to base a statement as to *what should be* upon a statement as to *what is*)" (*Grammar* 358). Christa Olson elaborates on Burke's definition by offering that "[c]onstitutions, thus, are particularly useful for Burke because they both act and authorize action; they set a scene and an attitude. Put another way, constitutions simultaneously make the conditions in which they function and shape orientations toward change." Sigma Chi and fraternities at Columbia have resisted change to a great degree by relying on both the histories of their organizations and the self-evident successes of brotherhood that are described in their constitutive documents like *The Norman Shield.* These documents enable fraternity members to identify as part of an enduring collective of males who occupy an important position in American life.

The documents do so by working on the fantasies of members to create a sense of chronology. As Michael McGee has pointed out, national collectives attain rhetorical weight through the "agreement of an audience to participate in a collective fantasy." That is, a collective of individuals see in a narrative of "the people" an identity they would like to share in, and consequently they each participate in imagining themselves as part of that collective. This identity carries with it a sense of the past, the present, and the future. McGee elaborates, "'the people' are more *process* than *phenomenon*. That is, they are conjured into objective reality, remain so long as the rhetoric which defined them has force, and in the end wilt away, becoming once again merely a collection of individuals." As visions of collective identity change, individuals go through a process of "coming-to-be, being, and ceasing-to-be an objectively real entity." This process, I submit, is often not made apparent through the rhetorical moves themselves; that is, often in the process of identifying as part of a collective, individuals are persuaded that they have always had particular qualities or interests in common with other members of the collective, even that traits such as character are inborn. Yet, in other moments, the process is on the surface of the rhetoric itself, wherein becoming is itself part of the narrative of identifying with a collective, though such narratives also often suggest that the identification, once achieved, is eternal. Fraternities are particularly focused on what they portray as the end-stage transition into collective adulthood, and therefore we see in documents from Sigma Chi, for example, a collective identity built around a narrative of becoming a particular kind of American man-in-the-making that exists on the surface, and even consciously performed through highlighting class distinctions in manners and dress.

The historical documents from Sigma Chi form one node of evidence of constitutive rhetoric that exists locally and enacts national identity through banal acts. National collective identification of the sort that McGee describes often takes place through daily acts of constitutive rhetoric. While Burke used the US Constitution as his representative anecdote for identification, attitudes and actions are induced by meaningful instances of identification as "the people" that occur daily and are mediated by documents of local groups, like the Columbia chapter of Sigma Chi.

And while the Sigma Chi handbook was written for a private audience and its rituals are secret, its acts of identification are perceivable in the broad descriptions of the organization in the handbook and in members' public statements. The handbook reached a national audience of Sigma Chi chapters, but members' acts of identification took place primarily within local chapters like the one at Columbia, within local contexts like the bias clause crisis in the 1960s, and within local performances such as the public statements members constructed for outsiders. The distinctions that members made between those fit to be members and those not fit were part of their processes of imagining their relationship to other men and to the United States. Michael Billig argues that in identification based on such distinctions, "[a] whole way of thinking about the world is implicated. If this way of thinking seems to be commonplace and familiar, then it, nevertheless, includes mystic assumptions which have become habits of thought" (61). These habits of thought include imagining the self—that is, identifying in ways that invoke an ideal in our most important relationships. We identify as members of a nation through the rhetorical processes that Burke, McGee, and Charland have elaborated on, while the "habits of thought" about national belonging that have grown from our "mystic assumptions" are cultivated quite influentially in organizations like college fraternities. These organizations accommodate the transformations necessary for a person to confront competing realities such as changes in the physical body and the need to support oneself in the US capitalist economy. Fraternities provide narrative possibilities for males to connect with broader, more abstract narratives such as that in the US Constitution through terms such as *ideals, brotherhood,* and *character.* As Billig argues, "small words, rather than grand memorable phrases, offer constant, but barely conscious, reminders of the homeland, making 'our' national identity unforgettable" (93). The practices of Sigma Chi at Columbia have the job of reminding members that they are members of the United States as a nation, but also that they are members of a particularly privileged kind, and that distinctions matter.

4

The Male Makeover and Emergent Masculine Identity in the "Army of One" Recruitment Campaign

IN CHAPTER 1, I DESCRIBE A *NEW YORK TIMES* column about the changing image of the ideal male figure on the fashion runway. This story focuses on a transformation in the image of the male, from a boyish form to a more masculine figure that the author explains is a response to economic shifts. In this chapter, I focus more extensively on a visual image of the male directed at graduating high school students who are potential recruits for the US Army. Here, the transition happens before the audience within the space of one recruitment brochure, and we see examples of "before" and "after," with the implication that the same will happen for all recruits during their training. As is the case with the Boy Scouts of America and Sigma Chi fraternity, the possibility of and need for transformation itself is the focus of the campaign's appeal to masculine identity.

In this chapter, I examine the rhetoric of masculine transformation nearly a century after the Boy Scouts of America was established, looking especially at the role images have played. As with the other organizations, I find contradictions in the US Army's rhetorical strategy. And again, Burke's analytical framework of identification is a crucial tool in helping me to understand the currency of the campaign and its compelling contradictions. While the use of visual rhetoric distinguishes the army campaign from the constitutive rhetorics of the BSA and Sigma Chi, the army pairs images with an origin myth of sorts that functions similarly as a scene to contain the act and actions it presents as following from that scene.

The US Army began its "Army of One" recruiting campaign in 2001. Spending an unprecedented figure on the effort, the army hired the advertising firm Leo Burnett, creator of McDonald's, Co-ca-Cola, and Visa campaigns, to develop a slogan and message. The campaign that evolved over the next few years employed several modes of communication to broadcast its appeal to youth and parents, including magazine advertisements, television commercials, an interactive website, video games, and brochures handed out by army representatives in recruiting offices and at recruiting events held at places of business, high schools, and college campuses. Officers drove Hummers painted with the "Army of One" slogan in local parades and parked them as an invitation to adventure at universities with high Hispanic enrollment. They set up rock climbing walls on wheels, challenging young men and women to confront their fears of falling while rock music poured from large speakers. And they handed out brochures that read as descriptions of a positive possible future in the army.

Despite these efforts to persuade youth to identify with the army, the campaign lasted only five years, far briefer than the prior twenty-year "Be All That You Can Be" campaign. During those five years, the United States experienced the September 11 attacks and the subsequent US wars in Afghanistan and Iraq, events the army could not foresee when it planned the recruiting strategy. Likely due in part to the threat and then reality of war, the army struggled to meet recruitment goals during the campaign. In 2006, after falling short of enlistees by the widest margin in more than two decades (Shanker), the military ended the "Army of One" campaign.

Though brief, the campaign represented a significant new multimodal approach to army recruiting that prompted the army to consider the values of its audience in more detail than ever before. The resulting visual and linguistic arguments to join the army were complicated by a tension between the collective identity of the army and the individual identity of the turn-of-the-twentieth-century young male (along with Americans more generally). This ambiguity, of course, would delight Burke, and I use his dramatistic model to explain this tension in the overall identity performance the campaign tried to establish. First, I recount the history of the campaign, which drew upon extensive government-sponsored research into youth values. Then I analyze two representative recruitment brochures that distill the message of the campaign into core concrete visual and linguistic appeals. Informed by a constitutive model of rhetoric and a visual model stemming in part from Roland Barthe's visual semiotic, I claim that the "Army of One" campaign's rhetoric of the makeover reveals an underlying narrative of emergent masculinity in which working-class young males of all races are naturally patriotic and in possession of an untapped masculine essence that can be transformed into full manhood through the army.

ARMY RECRUITING FROM THE MID-1990s TO THE PRESENT

The "Army of One" campaign developed in response to long-standing military recruitment problems. In 1973, President Nixon followed through with his campaign pledge to end military conscription, beginning the era of an all-volunteer military. In the mid-1990s, the military began facing severe recruiting challenges that have continued to the present, particularly in the case of the army. To meet its quotas, the army lowered its standards for the recruits it accepted: between the mid-1990s and 2002, the number of army enlistees scoring above the fiftieth percentile on the armed forces qualification tests had fallen by a third, and in the four-year period between 1998 and 2002, the army more than doubled the number of recruits it accepted with felony arrests (Moskos 78). These ongoing issues of numbers and standards for recruits led the Clinton and George W. Bush administrations to conduct research on the causes.

At the request of the US Department of Defense, in 2003 the National Research Council (NRC) produced a report titled *Attitudes, Aptitudes, and Aspirations of American Youth: Implications for Military Recruitment* (though it made the document available in draft form earlier). Bringing together data from a range of studies over the course of two decades, the report shaped the evolving rhetoric of the "Army of One" campaign. The authors found that the primary obstacles to recruitment were high college enrollment, the healthy economy, and decreased interest in the military (1). The findings shaped the exigency the army perceived during the course of the campaign.

The authors of the report were academics, business professionals, and retired military officers who consulted research on the life goals of high school seniors from 1976 to 1998. The data they studied demonstrated that high school seniors assigned the highest importance ratings to "finding purpose and meaning in my life," with more than 50 percent of males and 65 to 70 percent of females assigning the highest value to this category over the course of the study's twelve years (NRC 153). The authors wrote that "if military service in future years can provide such opportunities—and be perceived as doing so—the appeal is likely to be strong" (152). According to the report, youth who demonstrated a low propensity to enlist also reported strong skepticism about maintaining personal freedom in the military. The army addressed this finding by constructing a portrait of youth who were looking for purpose and meaning as free individuals and then suggesting that the army could provide that purpose and meaning as a singularly transformative experience, to be defined independently by each army member.

The report also found that youth patriotism had declined. The authors cite evidence that youth had little interest in national politics, low voting rates in national and congressional elections, and little accurate knowledge about national political processes, and that they "are the most bored and least engaged when they are attending history classes" (NRC 154). Those youth who were politically engaged,[1] according to this report, tended to focus on what they labeled "global issues" of human rights and global poverty, discrimination, disease eradication, animal rights, and environmentalism. The authors argue that these issues are "worldwide, not national" (155). The data imply that the majority of surveyed youth did not expect to find life purpose and meaning in domestic politics or patriotism. The youth in the study showed a fair amount of support for the statement that "the U.S. should be willing to go to war to protect its own economic interests," but less support for the statement that the United States should go to war to "protect the rights of other countries" (178–79).

Based on these data, the NRC report recommended that the army instill in youth a sense of patriotism and adventure and convince them that these two values are "best attained in the military" (NRC 216). The committee found that using advertising to educate youth on "the noble virtues of service to one's country" would ultimately increase enlistment because those who showed a high propensity to enlist also placed great importance on duty to country, and conversely, those who showed a low propensity to enlist placed low importance on duty to country (233–34).

In the end, the army attempted to pair this value of "duty to country" with the value for individual purpose and life meaning while at the same time emphasizing the opposite value of collective identity. This contradiction may have hobbled the rhetoric of the campaign, failing to convince youth to risk their lives in the army during the US wars in Afghanistan and Iraq that developed during the "Army of One" campaign. In Burke's terms, the unresolved ambiguity between the values of individualism and collective membership stands out—a point that I take up later.

Finally, the report states that a significant obstacle to military recruiting is the lack of academic success among Hispanics. I will note that the term *Hispanic* is not specific or preferred by many Latino/as and others from Spanish-speaking backgrounds, nor by academic writers generally, because it includes a widely diverse group of people that is not clearly defined; however, it is the term the report used and that the US government often uses. I cite the term here with skepticism about its usefulness in describing a group of people and therefore have doubts about the usefulness of the data the report connects to those it terms *Hispanics*. When analyzing other sources, I use the terms *Latino/a* and *Latino/as*.

Latino/as are the fastest growing demographic of young adults in the United States and will represent about 22 percent of eighteen-year-olds by 2020.[2] Yet, as a group, they have a relatively low high school graduation rate, and the military typically requires enlistees to have high school diplomas or GEDs (NRC 254–55). These statistics were particularly troubling for the military at the turn of the twenty-first century because they were coupled with a concurrent decrease in African American and female recruits (Lovato 16).[3] These observations about demographics had been noted during the Clinton administration and led to the passage of the Hispanic Access Initiative Act (HAIA) in 1996. HAIA allowed ROTC recruiters to target colleges and universities with sizeable "Hispanic" populations (Moran) such as the University of Arizona (a "Hispanic Serving Institution"), where I observed some of the military recruitment described earlier in this chapter. Beyond college campuses, the military used GIS maps to set up recruiting using souped-up Hummers (military sports utility vehicles) and presentations at Chuck E. Cheese restaurants in Latino/a neighborhoods, targeting Latino/a youth and their parents in the Southern California, Sacramento, and Phoenix areas (Lovato 14). The images in the "Army of One" recruiting brochures implied opportunity in the army regardless of race in order to appeal to a Latino/a audience.

The branches of the military used the data from the NRC report to argue successfully for Congress to pass immense budget increases directed toward recruiting. Before the report, between 1993 and 2000, the amount the military spent on advertising had increased 318 percent, yet with no notable increase in the propensity of young adults to enlist (NRC 226–27). Between 2000 and 2005, using the NRC report to support its argument to Congress for more funds, the army doubled its spending yet again, focusing on the "Army of One" campaign that began in 2001. In short, the army had a great investment in the success of its campaign. The army's consultants chose to offer recruits a narrative about their transformation into men—in the words of US Army Advertising Director Colonel Thomas Nickerson, the "Army of One" slogan "promotes personal success"—that included a ritualized statement of identity in the form of a creed, along with before and after images of what becoming an American man would look like. While both men and women appear in the campaign's recruiting brochures, the majority of figures are males and, I argue, the campaign draws on existing discourse on masculinity to construct its appeals. We see appeals to masculinity in all of the materials discussed in the following section, but most prominently in the Warrior's Creed.

RECRUITING DOCUMENTS

In the analysis that follows, I focus on two recruiting portfolios I was given at an army recruiting office in Tucson, Arizona, in 2006, at the campaign's end. These materials contain text, but they are filled most noticeably with digitally edited images. The cover of the first brochure (Figure 4.1) features a grainy, sepia-toned photograph of approximately ten young people the age of high school graduates standing in two rows with their right hands raised as if they are taking an oath. They are dressed in casual, loose-fitting street clothes and athletic shoes, with shirts untucked. The male in front has markedly poor posture. While the faces of at least two females are apparent, the majority of figures, including those at the front of each line, are male. Most appear light-skinned, though the sepia tones make it difficult to discern skin color. The floor they stand upon is shiny and reflects their profiles, and behind them hangs a large wavy fabric with wide stripes, which a US audience is likely to read as an American flag. The setting appears to be a gymnasium, a familiar representation of a high school, and along with the other elements of the photo, the association emphasizes the figures as young and directionless students.

Superimposed on the middle of this sepia-toned photograph is a smaller, more focused black-and-white photograph. In this inset, we see four young males and females lined up shoulder to shoulder, in sharp contrast to those lined up in the larger background photo. These figures wear crisp dress uniforms and serious, determined expressions on their faces. Their hair is close-cropped but not in a stereotypical military buzz cut, they have spotless complexions, and they stand with upright posture. Three of the soldiers appear light-skinned alongside one dark-skinned woman.

The placement of the smaller photo in the center of the larger photo directs the audience to make comparisons. In contrast to the inset photo, the young adults in the background photo look sloppy, slouchy, and young. The photo of the soldiers with straight posture connotes activity and assertiveness compared to the photograph of the students in the background, which connotes passivity. This contrast between the two photographs is emphasized

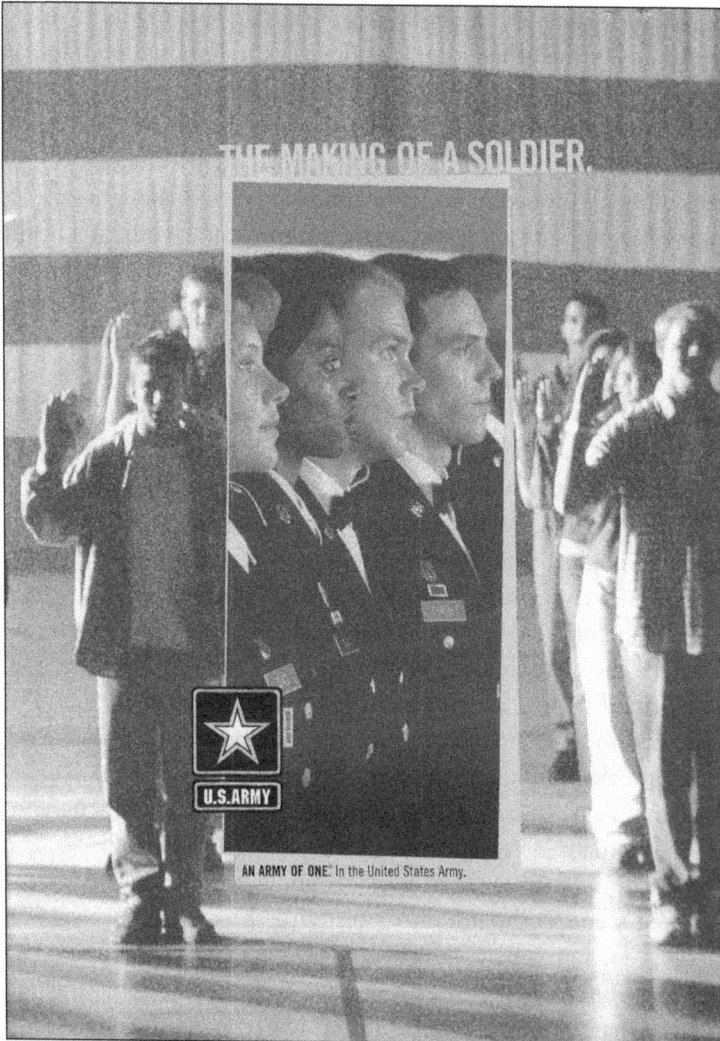

Figure 4.1. Cover of "The Making of a Soldier" army brochure.

by their geometry. The lines of the background photo are asymmetrical; the students' postures, their clothing, their disparate body heights and haircuts, and the diagonal, crossing lines on the floor created by the shadows and glare from a light source on the left all stand out against the straight lines of the flag hanging in the background. On the other hand, the lines of the imposed photograph are symmetrical. This photograph is placed in the center of the background photograph. We see two women and two men, all of the same height, with similar short hair, eyes all looking in the same direction, all dressed in the same uniform, all with straight posture and heads upright at the same level. A horizontal white line in the background, about one centimeter above the heads of the soldiers, emphasizes that each of these soldiers is the same height. The one feature of visual asymmetry about the inset photograph is the dark-skinned woman, but the darkness of her skin is mitigated by the low contrast of the photograph. The connoted message is multilayered. While the photographs suggest possibilities for the reader to "measure up," the symmetrical lines suggest a homogenizing effect in the army. This homogenizing connotation is supported by the denoted linguistic message of the slogan, "An Army of One"—and in reference to the image, the "One" suggests sameness.

The rhetoric of these two images takes place in the interaction between the connoted and the denoted messages, which creates an overall pull toward identification for a young male audience. The linguistic message presented alongside the image has a naturalizing effect on the connoted message of the image; as Roland Barthes explains, such "discontinuous connotators" in an image "are connected, actualized, 'spoken' through the syntagm of the denotation, the discontinuous world of symbols plunges into the story of the denoted scene as though into a lustral bath of innocence" (162). Because for Barthes the flow of language is part of a relational system that mimics speech, he argues that we read text as natural and transfer that naturalness to the image. The text and the image form "blocks of meaning," the assemblage of which is a rhetorical act, according to Charles A. Hill and Marguerite Helmers (17). As Barbie Zelizer explains, the elements of "subjectivity, voice, and contingency" give rhetorical meaning to visual representations (qtd. in Hill and Helmers 17).

This concept of the interaction between words and images helps explain how the army brochure operates rhetorically to constitute

subjectivity. The yellow text above the superimposed photo naturalizes the image and induces an audience to read the photo as evidence of a process of becoming: the yellow words above the superimposed photo say "THE MAKING OF A SOLDIER." However,
as Gunther Kress and Theo van Leeuwen have pointed out, the image is "an independently organized and structured message" with its
own grammar, independent of the linguistic text, and it persuades
us to create a story from it (18). The brochure's image prompts us
to understand a story of becoming that is not dependent on the
text: this is a makeover story.

The story-making effect of photos is rhetorical because viewers
bring their own context to the act of viewing and thus to story-
making; as Helmers argues, "'Just looking' is never innocent, nor is
it ever final" (65). More specifically relevant to the army brochure,
in reading, we inject images with a temporality, and we "extend
that which is limited by a frame to a before and an after" (Alberto
Manguel qtd. in Helmers 67). We are so culturally guided to see the
army as a transformative space, and to see a transformation from
boys to men, that we understand the two photos to depict a before-
and-after makeover story.

This makeover story is supported by elements within the images. The title reinforces the message in the images, but the image
itself is a story about transformation from the people in the grainy,
asymmetrical, sepia-toned photo to those in the clearer, symmetrical, grayscale photo. Black-and-white and sepia photographs have a
time-bound quality and emphasize the distance between an observ-
er and the photograph, while at the same time carrying a nostalgic
quality. They take advantage of what Barthes calls the "having been
there" quality of photographs. Viewers do not so much imagine
they are there as imagine that someone has been there and recorded
the event they are seeing. Because sepia tones are generally found
in very old photographs or photographs that are made to appear
old, the sepia tones here signify that the slouchy youths lined up in
this photo are from the past, and the newer, more focused grayscale
photo is recent.

Through the unique informational economy of photographs, the story takes on a quality of documentation. The frame within a frame presents a double reality of identities from two different points in time. Were this the medium of film, the story might be represented as a montage of images set to music showing the steps involved in the making—and the becoming—of a soldier. In the medium of the brochure, we see a hint that we are getting only the first and last frames of the montage in the uneven yellow marking surrounding the inset "after" photo, which suggests there are more photos underneath that document the "between" stages. The signs of before and after here reach into the genre of the makeover trope, a genre made omnipresent in American popular culture through programs as diverse as reality show *What Not to Wear* and the series *Spartacus,* and in films that use montage to show warrior-like transformation, such as *Rocky, The Matrix, District 9,* and even Disney's *The Sorcerer's Apprentice.* The title "The Making of a Soldier" anchors the image in this makeover, connoting the story of how the young people in the old photo were made into the purposeful adults, the "Soldiers," in the new photo. The movement from asymmetry in the background photo to symmetry in the foreground photo connotes a move from a directionless state to purposefulness for students who enlist. Clearly, the more appealing way to be is portrayed in the smaller inset photo; clearly, becoming a soldier is the direction toward purposefulness.

Inside the front cover of the brochure we find the words "AN ARMY OF ONE" and below, the phrase "AN ARMY OF ONE. YOU CAN SEE MY STRENGTH" (Figure 4.2). The connoted message tells us that strength (and, together with the visual and linguistic message described earlier, we might read personal growth) is visual, something that can be appreciated by looking at the surface of a person, thereby reinforcing the reliability of the photograph and the story it tells. So the message is that the difference readers see between the two photos is a difference of strength. Streaming down the center of the page, we read, "Even though there are 1,045,690 Soldiers just like me, I am my own force. With technology, with training, with support . . ." At this point, the large

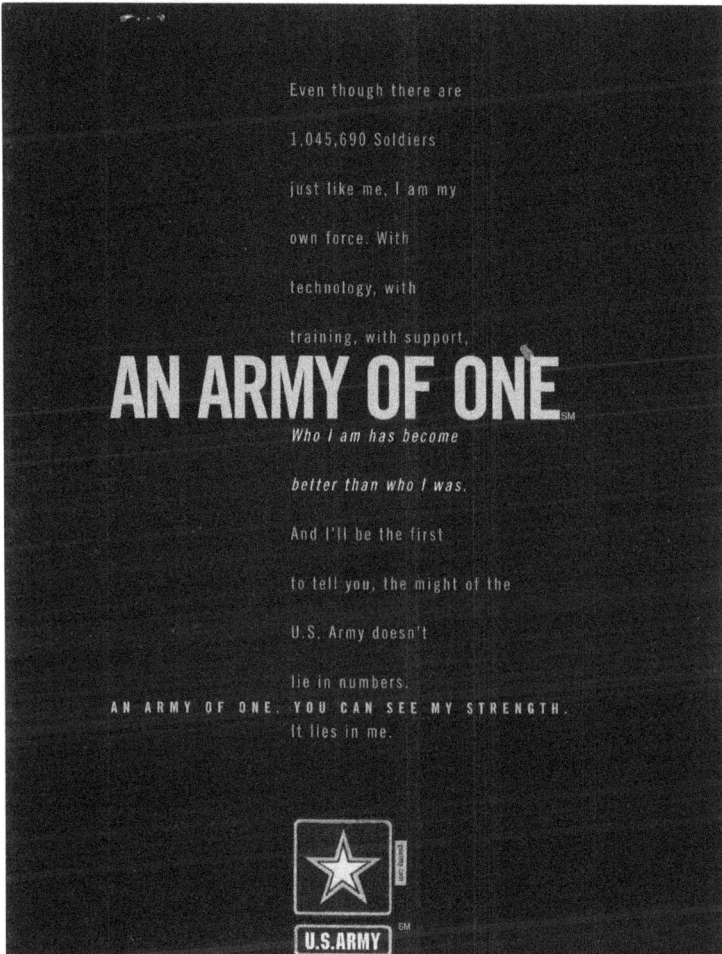

Even though there are

1,045,690 Soldiers

just like me, I am my

own force. With

technology, with

training, with support,

AN ARMY OF ONE℠

Who I am has become

better than who I was.

And I'll be the first

to tell you, the might of the

U.S. Army doesn't

lie in numbers.

AN ARMY OF ONE. YOU CAN SEE MY STRENGTH.
It lies in me.

U.S.ARMY

Figure 4.2. Inside front cover of "The Making of a Soldier" brochure.

yellow-type phrase "AN ARMY OF ONE" appears. The text continues in a medium-size typeface: "*Who I am has become better than who I was.* And I'll be the first to tell you, the might of the U.S. Army doesn't lie in numbers. It lies in me." Rhetoricians ask, who is the "me" these young soldiers have become? And how is it better? Young readers may see themselves as the "me," incorporating into their identities the familiar American myth of the American dream, manifested visibly. The document directs readers to these questions that arise from a sense of "after," or a possible future. As Hill and Helmers insightfully argue, drawing on Zelizer, this possible future is rhetorically potent:

> [W]ith . . . representational media, we are able to project "altered ends" for the representations we see. This insertion of the spectator's desires for the future is like the tense in verbal discourse, as tense can locate a moment into the past (that which has already happened and cannot be changed; visual *representation*), the present (what Zelizer terms the "as is"), or the future (the moment of possibility that Zelizer calls the "as if"). Rhetorically, "as if" has the greatest power because it directly involves the spectator and depends on the spectator's ability to forecast and manipulate contingencies in order to create a meaning. (17–18)

So in drawing its audience toward the future, the "as if," the brochure's images construct young adults as subjects.

This interaction between the image and the audience is part of the "hailing" relationship that Althusser describes and that I refer to in Chapter 1 (Helmers 68). The image becomes a narrative through the audience's process of seeing, and in seeing and creating that narrative, the audience also sees himself. In other words, the image hails the audience, and, as Althusser theorizes, the audience participates by seeing himself in the way that he imagines he is being seen. This is what Burke refers to as constituting the subject rhetorically. In this case, the constitutive rhetoric is visual, and I argue we should expand our conception of constitutive rhetoric to include the visual. Burke encouraged such an expansive view of symbolic media beyond text to include "mathematics, music, sculpture, painting, dance, architectural styles" (*Language* 28). The "Army of One" brochures continue the work of foundational documents in defining the "we" that is Americans.

While there are many signs operating in this advertisement, the process of becoming in the United States often carries as a subtext the rhetoric of the American dream and the Horatio Alger myth that a person can become successful on his own by working hard enough, two powerful forces for building identity among young people in the United States. Within this class-focused element of the brochures, a message about race also obtains, as the bootstraps myth relies on an erasure of the social function of race. For example, in the second photo, aside from skin color, everyone is physically similar, connoting similar opportunity for each of them. While the after image has the clearest presentation of visible race, it suggests that the discernable effects of race will be erased along with other weaknesses through the army's social makeover.

Three things about this text stand out as most persuasive, I would argue, even while they are among the subtler elements of the text. The first is that the word *Soldier* is always capitalized in this brochure. The second is that the text is written in first-person voice, though there is no obvious person who is speaking. The third is that in this short passage, a form of the word *me* is used seven times, while the word *Army* appears only three times. These elements centralize the individual, even in the context of joining the army collective. The focus on the individual is highlighted in the juxtaposition of numbers in the phrase "1,045,690 Soldiers just like me" and phrases that de-emphasize numbers and emphasize the individual, such as "The might of the Army doesn't lie in numbers," "It lies in me," and "I am my own force." This focus on the individual is also reflected in the cover photo, where the soldiers have become quite literally more clearly defined, suggesting they are more clearly defined as individuals when they have become part of the army organization.

The capitalization of the word *Soldier* in the text implies that a soldier is not a common person; he is someone to be respected, a proper noun. Also, the capitalization suggests an individual soldier rather than one of a number of soldiers given that in English proper nouns like *President* are capitalized when referring to a particular president but not when referring to a category like presidents generally. In treating *Soldier* as a proper noun, the document suggests individual identity, supporting the other linguistic and visual indexes for individuality in the campaign.

The use of first-person voice in this advertisement, absent any picture of a person who could be assumed to be a narrator, suggests to a reader that it is his own voice, coming from his own interior monologue. If a reader accepts the voice as his own, then he also hears the narrative as his own narrative. The message is a positive one as we see in phrases such as "I am my own force" and "[The might of the US Army] lies in me," and it reflects popular self-improvement dialogue, prompting readers to identify with the narrator and see the narrative voice as their own voice. A reader sees that this is not a brochure about the army or about "Soldiers"; rather, it is about himself. The text also brings up the constructed idea of "personal growth." In phrases such as *"Who I am has become better than who I was,"* value is placed on someone who has "become"—that is, someone who has joined the army rather than someone who has not.

While verbs in this brochure point to the transformation of an individual—the *making* of a soldier, who I *am*, who I *have become*—and the images reflect verbs, the overall campaign motto "Army of One" does not contain a verb, like the previous "Be All That You Can Be" campaign did. The action is joining the military. Once one joins, the brochure presents the transformation process as passive, something that happens because of belonging. But the collective belonging coexists with an emphasis on individuality.

This tension between the collective and the individual exposes an ambiguity in the relationship between the scene and the agent (and, by extension, the act). Military service is tied to individualism much more strongly than to collective nationalism in these materials. The message emphasizes being part of monumental history rather than just another member of the US nation or the military rank and file. This emphasis is apparent, for example, on the text of the next page:

> When you become a Soldier in the Army of One, you become part of a proud legacy stretching back more than 226 years. From George Washington's Continental Army, to the sands of the Middle East, the Army has served with pride and distinction. Soldiers have always done whatever it takes to get the

job done. They display a proud devotion to the tradition of professionalism and values passed down through the years. In the Army of One, you're not just part of an ordinary group, you're part of history.

The pride here is placed in a "tradition of professionalism," that is, pride in one's career rather than in the nation, and in being recognized through history—markers of individual achievement. The ambiguous relationship of the agent to the scene—is the agent an individual or part of a collective?—connects to the deeper historical tension between the ideal of the collective United States, embodied in the military, in organizations like the Boy Scouts, and in practices like reciting the Pledge of Allegiance and singing the National Anthem, always performed collectively, and the emphasis on individuality that has concurrently informed the rights protected in the US Constitution and in the capitalist marketplace and the myth of the self-made man. This tension arose with the BSA, as noted in Chapter 2 and with Sigma Chi and its tension between the concepts of discrimination and equality. The tension is one that characterizes youth organizations for boys in the United States and points to the crises these organizations experience. If we judge the images I have presented here (as a representation of the "Army of One" campaign) according to Sonja Foss's guidelines for rhetorical analysis of visual images ("Rhetorical Schema" 217), then their success in achieving their function or goal would be central. And on that basis, I would posit that the campaign was not as effective as it might have been if it had been able to resolve the ambiguity between the collective and the individual identities it offered its audience.

My purpose, however, is to connect the rhetorical appeals of the US Army to identification, and identification is not the same as effectiveness. As I mentioned in Chapter 1, the idea of effectiveness comes from what Greene calls the influence model of rhetoric, a model that relies on Aristotle's categories of persuasion. While the campaign may not have produced the recruitment the army had intended, and in that sense it failed to influence its intended audience, its message was disseminated widely. The relevant question for me is what and how subjectivities were made possible by the campaign. To answer this question, I consider how a scene was created for the ad that drew from a ritualized creed, in the same way that the origin myths and creeds of the BSA and Sigma Chi created a scene for their members.

THE SOLDIER'S CREED

The images in the "Army of One" brochure reflect the report the NRC produced for the Department of Defense. The army's attempt to create young males' identification through its campaign become clearer when the brochure is compared with a second brochure that was disseminated at the same time from the same army recruiting office. This second brochure is similar to the first, with three subtle but important exceptions (Figure 4.3). First, the inside cover of the second brochure has a different picture and text. The text, set against a black background, includes the title "The Soldier's Creed," followed by the text that army soldiers are required to learn in training. This version of the creed was adopted in 2003 and is a revision of the original Soldier's Creed:

I am an American Soldier.
I am a Warrior and a member
of a team.
I serve the people of the
United States and live the Army Values.
I will always place the mission first.
I will never accept defeat.
I will never quit.
I will never leave a fallen comrade.
I am disciplined, physically and
mentally tough, trained and proficient
in my Warrior tasks and drills.
I always maintain my arms, my equipment
and myself.
I am an expert and I am a professional.
I stand ready to deploy, engage, and
destroy the enemies of the United States
of America in close combat.
I am a guardian of freedom and the

American way of life.
I am an American Soldier.

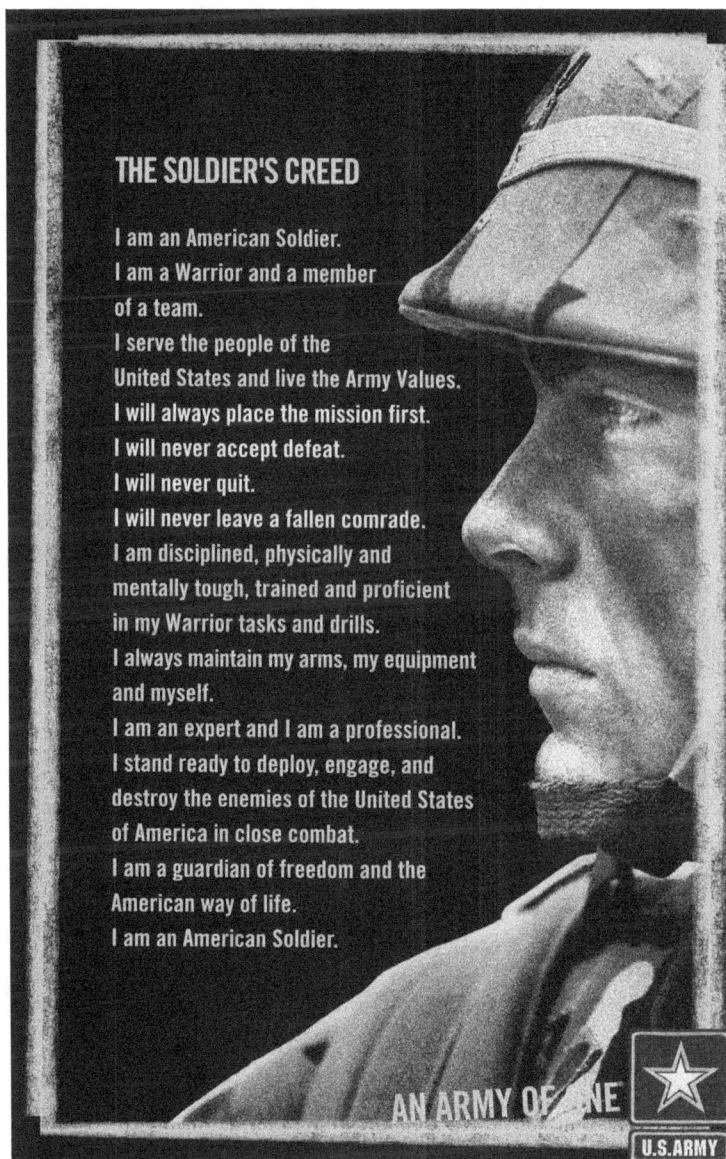

Figure 4.3. Cover of "The Soldier's Creed" brochure from the "Army of One" campaign.

To the right of the text, we see a large black-and-white picture of a male soldier's face and upper body in profile. The soldier wears a helmet and fatigues, with a rifle slung over his shoulder, and he looks forward with a serious expression. This is a soldier who is ready for combat. The picture is grainy enough that it is difficult to tell if it is a photograph or a drawing. This graininess allows for anonymity in the sense that the soldier could look like a range of males, so the image makes it possible for a male reader to imagine himself as the soldier. The soldier's eyes stare at and direct the viewer's attention to a section of the creed that stands out in white lettering against the black background. This section of the creed is called the "Warrior Ethos Statement":

I will always place the mission first.
I will never accept defeat.
I will never quit.
I will never leave a fallen comrade.

Through the combination of the soldier's gaze and the white text that separates these words, the image suggests that the soldier is thinking this particular section of text as he goes about his combat mission. As an agent, the soldier appears consistent with the post-makeover scene of American manhood in the first brochure.

The "Warrior Ethos Statement" presents the agent in a post-makeover state, transformed into a version of the American man. The statement itself is one of the many recent revisions to the Soldier's Creed (Burlas) and is a key part of identification the creed encourages through performance. Comparing the complete text of the new creed with the text of the previous creed, one can see a change of focus. The text of the old creed reads:

I am an American Soldier.
I am a member of the United States Army—a protector of the greatest nation on earth.
Because I am proud of the uniform I wear, I will always act in ways creditable to the military service and the nation it is sworn to guard.
I am proud of my own organization.

I will do all I can to make it the finest unit in the Army.

I will be loyal to those under whom I serve.

I will do my full part to carry out orders and instructions given to me or my unit.

As a soldier, I realize that I am a member of a time-honored profession—that I am doing my share to keep alive the principles of freedom for which my country stands.

No matter what the situation I am in, I will never do anything, for pleasure, profit, or personal safety, which will disgrace my uniform, my unit, or my country.

I will use every means I have, even beyond the line of duty, to restrain my Army comrades from actions disgraceful to themselves and to the uniform.

I am proud of my country and its flag.

I will try to make the people of this nation proud of the service I represent, for I am an American Soldier. (US Army)

The original creed emphasizes pride, restraint, and self-control in the service of the larger collective of the country. The speaker of the old creed is subservient to the country and the organization to which he belongs. Dependent clauses such as "Because I am proud of the uniform I wear" and "As a soldier" create an indirect tone that is passive in comparison to the tone of the new creed.

The revision of the creed, I believe, is the source of some of the ambiguity in the identification the "Army of One" campaign encouraged. The new creed refocused identity toward the abstraction of "warrior," an identity that was at odds with an identity focused on individuality. The new version of the creed was approved on November 24, 2003 (Kimbrell), to reflect changes in the military toward an emphasis on what the army calls its "Warrior Ethos." According to army officials, the "Warrior Ethos Statement" was part of the army's efforts to move army soldiers toward a "warrior mindset" (Burlas). Brigadier General Benjamin C. Freakley explains that the goal of the army is to get soldiers to think of themselves as warriors rather than as cooks, infantrymen, and postal clerks. He wanted army soldiers to think of themselves as "warriors and members of a team" despite coming from diverse backgrounds. He also explains that the goal is to change the culture of the army so that soldiers "examine [their] beliefs from a warrior's perspective," and to ensure that the army "produces and retains Soldiers of value to the nation" (Burlas). This shift to the warrior perspective coincides with the beginning of the US war in Iraq and reflects the military's focus on fighting abroad rather than on the domestic duties of the armed forces. It also represents an attempt to refocus the portrait of a soldier as an individual, as suggested by the "Army of One" campaign, so that the individual is synonymous with warrior—that is, an individual disciplined and directed toward fighting for the nation.

In the words of army representatives, the "Warrior Ethos Statement" reflects

the soldier's selfless commitment to the nation, mission, unit, and fellow soldiers. It is the professional attitude that inspires every American soldier. Warrior ethos is grounded in refusal to accept failure. It is developed and sustained through discipline, commitment to the Army values, and pride in the Army's heritage." (LaMotte)

The Warrior Ethos relies on what Theodore Adorno calls an "ideology of hardness," reflecting, in the words of Henry Giroux, a "pathological relationship with the body" and a tendency toward pain—in other words, a hypermasculinized individual (60). This pathology forms the cultural basis for the Warrior's Creed. The creed remains rooted in a narrative of transformation but places that transformation in the service of the army collective rather than an individual identity that extends beyond the army.

"ARMY OF ONE" AS CONSTITUTIVE RHETORIC

As I have asserted, appeals to a masculine identity, either "pre-" or "posttransition," defined the "Army of One" campaign. These identity appeals included sophisticated marketing tools that addressed potential recruits as future workers, adventure seekers, and family members as well as soldiers. The 2001 campaign was an attempt by the army to use a variety of survey data to create an appeal to a sense of purpose and life meaning for the young adults it would recruit, in large part by tying that purpose and meaning to a transition to masculinity. The campaign aimed to link inchoate individual identity to military service by presenting the army as a group of common individuals, mostly male, who have undergone personal transformations into successful, exceptional American men. But this attempt to influence American male youth to identify with the army may have been hampered by its ambiguities in the scene-agent ratio.

As with the BSA and the Sigma Chi fraternity, the "Army of One" campaign can best be understood as a constitutive rhetorical appeal in the sense that it communicates a story about the individual. While in traditional Aristotelian models rhetoric is bounded by existing "conviction and convention," as Thomas Farrell has written—in other words, appealing to who people believe themselves to be—a view of rhetoric as constitutive finds rhetoric to be capable of creating "essentially novel and even unprecedented modes of consciousness and affiliation" (325). Constitutive rhetoric creates a consciousness among people of who they are, a subjectivity. As Maurice Charland elaborates, rhetoric can and must enjoin people as a collective, giving them a shared identity that allows them to then be collectively persuaded. As a constitutive force, rhetoric can create conditions for new means of persuasion through identification rather than merely finding those that exist (Jasinski 106).

As I noted in the Chapter 1, several studies have demonstrated the role of identity appeals in motivating audiences toward collective action. As Helen Tate has argued, however, these studies have tended to elide the cultural and historical complexities that can attenuate or change constitutive rhetoric over time (8). In contrast to national projects of constitutive rhetoric such as those that Charland has explicated, the army did not attempt to constitute a national collective with a single purpose and vision. Rather, the army directed its audience's identification toward a collective of individuals, with an emphasis on realizing and preserving individualism through the collective space of the army.

What would individuality look like for newly graduated male teenagers? And who are these imagined newly graduated teenagers? Outside of the stereotypes of the first-year college student, the years that encompass a chronological shift from teenager to young adult do not find many analogs in the collective consciousness. The army attempts to fill this lacuna in popular representation by offering a symbolic means of transformation, a bridge across which recruits can travel from the known world of adolescence to the known world of independent young adulthood. Independent young adulthood is presented as a vague notion of confidence, togetherness, and poise, along with the physical and character strength suggested by the warrior image. The liminal space before this stage would seem to be a perfect scene for constitutive rhetoric. In the same way that "'the people' are more a process than a phenomena," as McGee claims, the recruits are a process. Through constituting teens' subjectivity around this process of becoming, the "Army of One" campaign outlined a subject who has both become an individual and become part of the collective machine of the army, presenting the two identities as simultaneous and without paradox, eliding a contradiction in the larger American mythos. The army had to overcome a cultural perception of the army as a space that quells individuality, demands conformity, and defines a successful soldier as one who has had his individuality broken.

In attempting to persuade youth that they could develop their individual identities in the army, the campaign offered a message that juxtaposed individual identity with collective identity without reconciling these contradictions. The campaign received public criticism for this seeming contradiction. For example, a 2001 *New York Times* article pointed to it:

It might seem incongruous for the Army, which for two centuries has trained its recruits in the art of selflessness and unit cohesion, to promote itself as an incubator of self-actualization. Indeed, in recent decades many military officials have come to view the armed forces as a redoubt against unbridled individualism. (Dao)

A Vietnam veteran asked in a *Times* editorial, ". . . one what? Since when was the Army about individuality? When, except in those silly Rambo movies, was it about anything except group unity and sacrificing personal wants for the common good?" (Haberman). For many, the campaign did not escape the army's long-standing symbolism of collective identity, nor did it successfully explain how one could be both "one" and part of a collective within the army.

Yet the idea of individualism from "those silly Rambo movies" seems to be exactly what the army was suggesting it would provide. The phrase "Army of One" did not originate with the army; it was the title of the 1999 DVD release of an action film starring Dolph Lundgren as a rebel hero who breaks out of prison, takes an attractive woman hostage, and drives at high speeds across the desert and through Los Angeles in order to evade authorities. By drawing from an action movie title, the army invited the audience to see the army as a space for lone rebels who act independently to save the day rather than those who act out of loyalty to a group or nation.

By the second half of the campaign, the army attempted to address the contradictions of its scene-agent ratio by qualifying the individualism it promoted. As described earlier, the army was motivated by the NRC report to increase the sense of patriotism among high school seniors. It follows that the army would need to constitute youth as part of a national collective with a common destiny and purpose in order to persuade them that they should join, despite any individualism its campaign offered. The degree to which the campaign tied the dominant theme of individual "becoming" to the collective varied, depending on whether the brochure was printed before the publication of *Attitudes, Aptitudes, and Aspirations of American Youth* (NRC) or after. The 2001 brochure does not present overtly patriotic messages, and the inside of the cover contains first-person narrative text but no images. In the 2006 brochure printed at the campaign's close, the Soldier's Creed ties "becoming" to the image of the warrior, the soldier whose mental and physical discipline are directed toward serving the nation and supporting a team. In the picture of a soldier whose eyes look at the text of the Soldier's Creed in this later brochure, viewers see one soldier who could be any soldier. The voice of the creed, the "I" that begins each line, directs readers to understand the speaker as themselves. The image and text push the audience to imagine their potential individual identity as that of a warrior.

Rather than recharacterizing the army as a collective, the campaign recharacterized the picture of the individuals who join, and this picture of individuality took on new connotations once the army began sending soldiers to post-9/11 operations in Afghanistan and Iraq. Despite the other images in the brochures that show army enlistees working desk jobs, experiencing adventure, and connecting with family members (connotations that themselves became less meaningful or acquired different meaning once the US wars in Afghanistan and Iraq began), the cover and inside cover images of each brochure set the tone for the brochure and represent the predominant message of the campaign. As the US wars developed, it became difficult for any potential enlistee to imagine himself as an individual in the army without at the same time being conscious of images and news of the army's role in foreign military operations—and aware that an individual enlistee was bound to go to Afghanistan or Iraq.

This focus on the individual was also bound contextually by coverage of the wars that mediated the rhetoric of army numbers. Early in the operations, popular US news sources began announcing numbers of dead American soldiers. In reading recruitment phrases such as "Even though there are 1,045,690 Soldiers just like me, I am my own force," an audience might well have been reminded of the increasing number count in the daily news.[4] What would being "my own force" mean in the face of a rising death count?

In fact, individuality in the army was often tied in the mainstream media to descriptions of death. For example, on the nightly CNN network show *Nancy Grace,* the host began focusing each night during the "America Remembers" segment on an individual soldier who was killed, posting the deceased man or woman's photograph on the screen and mentioning his or her unique personality characteristics as recounted by friends and family in an attempt to put individual faces to the statistics. This type of honoring of fallen soldiers became increasingly common in the years after the military operations began and created a scene in which dying was part of the army experience. In public debates over the US wars, the link between soldier deaths and patriotism grew increasingly complex.

For example, though Grace referred to killed soldiers as "American heroes," soldiers in general were represented by antiwar rhetors as a collective underclass, directed by economic necessity into unwarranted violence, the result of misguided national policy.

As a term of identification for the campaign, then, individualism was fraught, fighting against a choice recruits had to make between army service and personal safety. The army's attempt to move its audience from "one 'world' of attitudes and conditions to another" (McGee) was countered by the world of attitudes and conditions that the mainstream media presented in its honoring of soldiers or contempt of the war. After 2003 it became more likely that potential recruits would believe that joining the army would mean agreeing to, in the words of Benedict Anderson, become part of a "deep, horizontal comradeship" that would require youth to be willing "not so much to kill, as willingly to die" for their nation (8). The narrative of personal becoming, of the masculine makeover, would have to overcome this meaning to move young males to join the collective project of war.

5

Using the Concept of Emergent Masculinity in the Rhetoric and Composition Classroom

> Subjectivity is not only composition, then; it is revision-in-movement, the combinatory woof and warp of singular, emergent events and belated, symbolic integrations. . . . Writing and subjectivity thereby resonate together. So perhaps, as writers, scholars, and teachers, we are all just writing our own escapes and thereby writing ourselves.
>
> —Thomas Rickert, *Acts of Enjoyment: Rhetoric, Zizek, and the Return of the Subject*

EMERGENT NATIONAL MASCULINITY IN THE CLASSROOM

IN THIS CHAPTER, I OFFER SOME APPLICATIONS of my argument about the rhetorics of emergent American masculinity to rhetoric and writing pedagogy. If, as Rickert argues in the chapter-opening excerpt, we are writing ourselves when we teach, then we must not attempt to separate our learning from that of our students. Collaboration with our students is especially important in a rhetoric class that aims to analyze sites of masculine national identification because we too are an audience for the rhetoric of emergent national masculinity; we live with gender and its intersections with nationalism and discursive and visual performance, just as our students do. This similarity means that we are well situated to work with our students as they become conscious of the influences on their sense of self and on their actions.

The analyses in this book might suggest the following pedagogical questions for rhetoric teachers: How are we to think about organizations like the BSA and their relationship to American male youth? How are we to imagine their relationship to the rest of us? What historical contradictions obtain in the organizations' stories, and how do these contradictions shape our ideas about men in the United States? Answering these questions along with students will require a struggle, though I believe a valuable one. I agree with Brad Evans and Henry Giroux when they write,

> Pedagogy is, in part, always about both struggle and vision— struggles over identities, modes of agency, values, desires, and visions of the possible. . . . Thus, education is by definition a form of political intervention. . . . The world that we inhabit . . . educates [Americans] of the need for warfare; it prizes, above all, the values of militarism and its conceptual apparatus of "civic soldierology." (8)

A course in rhetorics of emergent American masculinity would direct students to critically engage this militarism and "civic soldierology" by examining the documents that organizations for boys have produced, applying a rhetorical lens that will help them to make reasoned arguments.

A note on how my politics influence this pedagogical approach: these organizations for boys emerge from a nexus of psychological, social, historical, and political needs, some of which I have described in previous chapters. While American youth organizations for males draw from myth to serve specific political purposes, I contend that it is not possible or even desirable for boys to avoid entirely incorporating myths into their identities. Despite my own personal disagreement with the BSA's historical position on gay membership and leadership, the "Army of One" campaign's recruitment of young men for a cause I find disingenuous, and the history of elitism, sexism, and racism in college fraternities, I have come to understand through my research that these organizations address a persistent need among young American men to build an identity as they live within the demands of American culture and economic survival, dynamic as both of these factors are. For this fundamental reason, I argue that the most useful pedagogical approach we can take is to engage students in an understanding of why such organizations, myths, recruiting tactics, and creeds appeal to so many of us and how they fit into a historical context. We can learn quite a bit from our students about the way these organizations influence identities and lives, and together with our students we can consider how we might best think and act based on this understanding, particularly given the gender, racial, economic, and national diversity of most student populations. I offer a framework for approaching the rhetoricality of national masculine institutions and organizations and for problematizing them using Burkean analysis, a framework that can then be applied more broadly, but I do not offer an argument about whether students should join such institutions and organizations.

Pedagogical questions arose early during my research for this monograph because my students have been within the population that emergent masculinity accommodates. They may have been recruited by the military, they may have joined fraternities, or they may have risen through the ranks of the BSA not long before attending college. Those who grew up in the United States have negotiated the definitions of American masculine character that circulate among us all, and those who immigrated recently have been measured along with those who have internalized masculine identity over a long period of time and have likewise responded to demands to identify through gender performance. So our students are in an excellent position to consider how rhetorics of emergent masculinity are shaping them. The subject of male youth organizations provides a starting place for students to consider a range of rhetorical concepts and theories. In particular, rhetorics of emergent masculinity provide sites of analysis through which our students can explore contemporary rhetorical approaches focused on identity. Nationalism theories also demonstrate rhetorical identification as a function of everyday life.

THE COURSE: RHETORICS OF EMERGENT
MASCULINITY IN THE UNITED STATES
The course I describe in the following sections is particularly suited for upper-division undergraduate students, though it could be

adapted for graduate students who wish to engage more deeply with the theories I have drawn on in the previous chapters. Some of the basic concepts will also work for first-year undergraduate students if the materials are explicitly tied to a basic framework for academic writing or rhetorical analysis.

The Analysis Practice

The course examines three types of texts. The first is the origin myth. All of the organizations examined in this book function through a myth of their inception that relies on vague, apocryphal stories. Such stories provide fertile material for students to study the way a variety of historical, political, and economic motives can coalesce in US culture through origin stories.

The second type of text is the creed or oath. Such statements may be tied in an obvious way to national identity when they are part of a national organization or when they are inherently nationalist statements, as with the Pledge of Allegiance, but students can likely find other examples that intersect more closely with their daily lives.

The final type of text is the recruiting campaign image. While I have touched only the surface of visual rhetoric and its theoretical connection to semiotics here, rich possibilities exist for exploring national masculinity by analyzing popular, governmental, and commercial documents that contain images as part of campaigns, as well as physical sites such as monuments that are invoked in campaigns. Students can learn about the relationship between images and texts and study frameworks that help them to explain how the connoted and denoted messages encourage particular identity formations.

Theoretical Lenses

The course description I provide here is designed to help students frame their rhetorical inquiry around a set of documents and engage in informed analysis of the historical texts they uncover by applying a Burkean framework of rhetoric as identification. The course begins as a general inquiry into national rhetoric in the United States, gradually prompting students to narrow their focus to a site that might include the types of organizations I have studied here. It asks students to consider the role of language in an imagined common American identity, including the concepts of a shared past and common destiny. It leads students to the basic question of how we are persuaded to include some groups in our definition of *American* and exclude others. Students use Kenneth Burke's theory as a window through which they can carefully see the historical documents they read as constituting national and masculine identity.

Readings

The first reading in the course is Lisa Lowe's "Immigration, Citizenship, Racialization: Asian American Critique," the introductory chapter to Lowe's book *Immigrant Acts: On Asian American Cultural Politics*. This chapter examines the tenuous space that Asian Americans have occupied as racialized Americans, prompting students to explore the relationship between language and national identity (and its overlap with race and gender). Lowe argues that remembering and forgetting are key to national identification, a theme that is repeated in many nationalist texts. Giving an account of the relationship between Asian immigration to the United States and US wars in Asia and backlash against Asian Americans through anti-immigration legislation in the United States, Lowe concludes that representations of mainstream American identity have depended on exclusion and that alternative cultural expressions have emerged as a result of both that exclusion and inclusion in an American national identity. This complex treatment of national identity through the lens of race and class, drawing on a specific site such as the Vietnam Veterans Memorial, introduces concepts that this course will build on.

Students next read selections from Kenneth Burke's *A Grammar of Motives* and *A Rhetoric of Motives*, using his terms of the pentad that treat rhetoric as a performative yet sometimes unconscious act based on identification and occurring all around us every day. A guiding question during class discussion of Burke's theory is, how does Burke help us understand the relationship that Lowe sets up between language and American identity?

With a rhetoric vocabulary and a sense of the important questions that will arise in the course, students then move to nationalism theory and defining the concept of "nation" and its relationship to language and image. Readings might include Ernest Renan's foundational article "What Is a Nation?," Anthony D. Smith's "The Origin of Nations," and Benedict Anderson's introductory chapter and "Census, Map, Museum" from *Imagined Communities: Reflections on the Origin and Spread of Nationalism,* among many other options from the texts I have examined in earlier chapters in this volume. The goal is to help students understand national identity as a construction, as well as understand how narratives of the past and of the future are used to construct our present sense of national identity with a common destiny. Class discussions focus on creating connections between Burkean rhetorical theory and nationalism, with examples provided as concrete bases for class discussion.

Next, readings in gender and masculinity theory begin with R. W. Connell's *Masculinities,* in which she defines *hegemonic masculinity* (37) as a "gender practice" (77), as I noted in Chapter 1. Selections from Gail Bederman's *Manliness and Civilization: A Cultural History of Gender and Race in the United States, 1880–1917* provide a historical frame for understanding white masculinity as constructed through texts in response to changing economic and cultural forces on white male identity in the United States. Dana Nelson's *National Manhood: Capitalist Citizenship and the Imagined Fraternity of White Men* and E. Anthony Rotundo's *American Manhood: Transformations in Masculinity from the Revolution to the Modern Era* also provide excellent resources for understanding the historical development of white masculinity in the United States.

At this point, the reading turns to Sonja Foss's essay "Ambiguity as Persuasion: The Vietnam Veterans Memorial." Now understanding rhetoric as an everyday performance that extends to a variety of media, the class can discuss Foss's analysis as an extension of Burke's concepts to encompass visual texts—in Foss's example, a monument. Foss provides a list of rhetorical characteristics she finds useful for analysis of a monument, and these characteristics provide a framework for students' analysis of visual documents generally.

She begins by defining a rhetorical response versus an aesthetic response to a visual object, with a rhetorical response being one that connects the object to events or people outside of the object itself. She lists the five features that distinguish the memorial, from which students can draw the following list of criteria for reading visual material, with the exception of number four: (1) whether the monument "violates the conventional form of war memorials," (2) whether "it assumes a welcoming stance," (3) how much information it provides to the visitor, (4) whether it focuses attention on those who survived the war or on those who did not, and (5) whether it "generates multiple referents for its visual components" (331–32). These criteria give students a framework for understanding how origin myths, creeds, and visual elements coalesce in an image.

With a foundation in rhetoric, nationalism, and hegemonic masculinity, students then move on to analyze and critique a variety of documents, beginning with origin myths, moving on to creeds and oaths, and finishing with recruitment campaign images. University archives and local museums are excellent sources for these materials. The chapters in this book can provide students with examples, and they will be able to provide many more sites for analysis themselves.

Course Goals
Students will learn a discourse to use to describe how texts work persuasively to construct identity and influence actions. They will become familiar with Kenneth Burke's definition of rhetoric and his pentadic model for analysis and begin to understand how to rhetorically analyze visual texts. They will apply Burkean rhetorical analysis to texts and images of emergent American masculinity.

Assessment
In this course, students are assessed based on classroom discussion and engagement with the readings, analytical aptitude demonstrated in written work, and application of the theory from the course to a research project. While the final projects can take a variety

of forms, from traditional research-based analysis paper to a video presentation, the projects will be assessed on how well they apply rhetorical analysis to a site of emergent masculinity.

Students are given two short (three- to five-page) analysis assignments requiring them to apply Burke's theory to, first, an organization's origin story and, second, an organization's creed or oath. Universities, fraternities, and other organizations typically post origin stories on the history page of their websites, and organizations such as the YMCA often have relationships with their surrounding neighborhoods and cities that are mythologized in these origin stories. Students might choose to focus on organizations for males, but those for female members provide rich material for analysis as well. Likewise, oaths and creeds are often posted online.

In a final project, students present an extended analysis of an organization or institution's recruitment campaign, analyzing both text and images associated with it. Students draw on primary documents along with the rhetorical, nationalism, and gender theory they have acquired during the semester. Students must include historical context to support their analysis of the way the documents create identification among audiences.

Syllabus and Reading Schedule

The Rhetoric of Emergent Masculinity in American Youth Organizations

This course will orient you to the rhetoric of masculinity as it has been shaped through youth organizations in the United States during the twentieth and twenty-first centuries. You will learn to apply a Burkean rhetorical framework in which identity is central to persuasion and performing our identities shapes our beliefs and actions. You will also explore how identity and identification have shaped the US concept of masculinity and also given rise to organizations that offer a path to boys who want to achieve American masculinity—in other words, a way to become "real men."

The course focuses on three strains of theory:

- Kenneth Burke's theory of rhetoric: a view of rhetoric as identification and a model of persuasion that focuses on the drama of human motives at play
- Nationalism theory: a collection of writings that argue in various ways that nations are as much imagined communities of diverse people as real legal and political entities
- Masculinity/gender theory: a set of articles and chapters that conceive of gender as a historically situated construction that helps shape our identities

Your work in the course will be to analyze three types of texts: origin myths, oaths or creeds, and recruitment documents.

Required Texts
- Course Packet

Supplementary Material
Additional articles and other documents will be available on the course website, including the following: Jones, Leigh A. "Emerging Masculinity as Rhetorical." 2015. MS.

Course Requirements
The course has three writing requirements: a 3- to 5-page analysis of a male youth organization's origin story; a 3- to 5-page analysis of a male youth organization's creed or oath; and a 10-page, research-based analysis of a recruitment campaign.

You are also required to keep a reading journal in which you record your responses to the readings and draw connections between them. I will collect your journal weekly.

Grading
Reading Journal: 10%
Analysis Paper #1: 20%
Analysis Paper #2: 20%
Research Project: 40%
Drafts: 10%

Schedule

Week 1: Introductions.
         Reading: Lisa Lowe's "Immigration, Citizenship, Racialization"
Week 2: Reading: Leigh A. Jones's "Coming of Age as a Boy in America"
Week 3: Reading: selection from Kenneth Burke's *A Rhetoric of Motives*
Week 4: Reading: selection from Kenneth Burke's *A Grammar of Motives*
Week 5: Reading: Ernest Renan's "What Is a Nation?"and Anthony D. Smith's "The Origin of Nations"
Week 6: Workshop on first analysis paper
         Reading: Benedict Anderson's introduction to *Imagined Communities*
Week 7: Due: First analysis paper
         Reading: Benedict Anderson's "Census, Map, Museum" and selection from R. W. Connell's *Masculinities*
Week 8: Reading: selection from Gail Bederman's *Manliness and Civilization*
Week 9: Workshop on second analysis paper
         Reading: selection from Anthony Rotundo's *American Manhood*
Week 10: Due: Second analysis paper
Week 11: Reading: selection from Dana Nelson's *National Manhood*
Week 12: Workshop on research project
         Reading: Sonja Foss's "Ambiguity as Persuasion"
Week 13: Individual conferences on research project
Week 14: Workshop on research project
Week 15: Due: research project

6

Reconsidering the Rhetoric That Moves "Boys" to Become "Men"

FROM AMONG THE REPRESENTATIVE ORGANIZATIONS presented in this book, common themes emerge. The organizations all draw from what I have referred to as a rhetoric of becoming a man: a set of language practices using oaths, mission statements, creeds, and handbooks to construct young males as subjects in the process of becoming hegemonic men who fill a key role in the nation. Burke's rhetorical theory helps explain how this rhetoric has functioned by establishing identity, and Burkean theorists help to tie this identification to a constitutive worldview. According to this rhetoric, males in these organizations will become men with distinctive values demonstrated by their characters. As I have demonstrated, however, these values are not identical for each organization. For example, the Boy Scouts of America construct the boy subject as "thrifty," while Sigma Chi fraternity places importance on exclusivity. The US Army in its "Army of One" recruiting campaign uniquely emphasized being tough rather than prepared, clean, or well mannered. In other words, there is ambiguity in any overarching national masculinist scene one might attempt to construct from these three examples.

Yet, taken together, a picture develops of a common American story about the role of organizations in forming the male subject in this country and its attendant story of transformation from boyhood to manhood. This story assumes that boys must be groomed through a connection to a larger national community that guides them, through language, toward fully becoming men. The language constructs a threat that without such guidance and associations, boys will fail to develop into true members of the nation physically, economically, and morally.

I do not mean to suggest that it is possible to exist outside of ideas about development of various kinds. Boys do change physically, psychologically, and emotionally as they age. However, I have asserted here that the language these organizations use to describe that aging is not accidental, nor is it reflective of any enduring reality about boys' development. It is part of a discourse that obtains cultural force through repeated rhetorical acts by motivated rhetors. The organizations in this study present this chronological change as a national drama in which boys are agents whose actions have significance beyond them, consequences that affect everyone who participates in imagining the American space. The tie between boys and the nation has been imagined in various ways for boys of various races, classes, ethnic backgrounds, and religions, though the sites in this book point to a dominant pattern of identification in which many Americans, male and female, have participated. Taken together, they demonstrate the complexity and multiple layers of young hegemonic male identification.

The BSA's rhetoric of identification reveals how young males drew on colonial narratives from Britain to explain race and male destiny in the United States. The narratives helped the boys to understand their development through the early twentieth century discourses of science and education. The history of the organization also reveals contradictory messages in the rhetoric. On the one hand, the Cub Scouts branch of the organization presented stories from Kipling's *The Jungle Book* to create a narrative about ideal boy behavior by which "boy" was synonymous with evolved whiteness. On the other hand, the organization professed to—and often did—accept members of many races, ethnicities, and religions. While racial tension is part of the history of troops and racial integration was far from seamless in the organization, the BSA has included troops for boys of a variety of backgrounds, all of whom used the same narratives to build identification with ideal boyhood and a process of evolving in the right direction as a boy moves toward manhood. Later in the twentieth century, the issue of sexuality among members and Scout leaders became a central part of the organization's evolution.

Through the documents of Sigma Chi fraternity, contradicting ideals of conformity and individualism constitute members' identities. Fraternities are commonly stereotyped as promoting conformism, and the Sigma Chi handbook and public statements from members at Columbia University over the last six decades support this idea. Yet the organization's origin myth is a story of rebellion against what it characterizes as an uncritical group mentality, praising individual merit instead of uncritical loyalty. In this sense, it is also a quintessentially American story that echoes the Horatio Alger narrative of reward for individual work or talent. But perhaps it is even more American in the alternative story it tells about conforming to an organization in order to identify as male within a system of subtle class hierarchies.

The "Army of One" campaign shares this contradiction between the collective and the individual. However, the US Army's origin story, the Soldier's Creed, offers an inverse moral in which the soldier's individuality is overcome by loyalty to the organization. In this story, a soldier develops his commitment to his fellow soldiers as he becomes a man. The Soldier's Creed exists in tension with the campaign's first-person appeals promising to develop a soldier as an individual.

These different rhetorical appeals to becoming masculine, examined through an identificatory, constitutive rhetoric, deepen the picture gender theorists have painted of the development of masculinity in the United States. We know that the history of masculinity is bound by a transformation at the turn of the twentieth century in social relationships between white people and people of color, between men and women, between new immigrants and citizens, between the working class and the wealthy, and between the newly wealthy and those with more firmly established wealth. The narrative of masculinity consolidated insecurity among white men through colonial discourse from England and scientistic discourse about gender and race. What we have ample opportunity to explore is how this discourse manifested in particular cases, and how it was enacted through systems of identification on a daily basis across the country. This book points to the role of origin stories in establishing a history for the rhetorical construction of masculinity, a history that positions male subjects as inevitable. This imagined history precludes an awareness of the rhetorical process in which subjects are participating. That is, it suggests that the organizations are part of the natural march of history. Other documents suggest that members' development as men in a particular way is also part of the natural march of history.

I have referred to the organizations in this book as representative because they contain narratives about development that we can find elsewhere. If the narratives in these sites have lasting cultural power, it is because they are repeated again and again and influence perceptions of masculinity and manhood among nonmembers. This study leads to new questions about the function of constitutive rhetoric in banal American practices that create young masculine identity, pointing to a need for further rhetorical studies. Perhaps the most obvious question that emerges is, given the history of the Boy Scouts of America, Sigma Chi fraternity, and the US Army's recruitment campaigns, how might we understand the ways in which the rhetoric of becoming a man circulates around other young male organizations in contemporary life? There are many possibilities for further study, including the Civil Air Patrol, the YMCA, and Pop Warner football leagues, to name just a few.

Another question that bears further research by rhetoricians is how American organizations continue to constitute and reconstitute male identity at later stages in a man's life. For example, how do organizations like the Freemasons, the Knights of Columbus, the Veterans of Foreign Wars, and other community organizations create their members as agents who have already "become" men? How do these organizations negotiate members' aging as a part of masculine identity?

Also worth further consideration is the distinction between the organizations in this book and organizations targeted at young males of color, immigrants, or non-Protestant white groups, some of which claim to cater to males of all races, religions, and ethnicities, and some of which expressly have offered membership only to straight, white, and/or Christian males. The BSA, for example, has claimed since its founding to be open to all boys regardless of race, religion, or creed. However, the organization until very recently prohibited gay boys and men from becoming members or leaders. Do organizations that offer an alternative space for young males of marginalized groups also employ a rhetoric of becoming as a source of identification for members? How is this rhetoric different from the rhetorics that appear in the organizations described in this book? A related question is what happens when members cross the race, ethnicity, language, or sexuality boundaries that are established in the rhetorics of mainstream male youth organizations?

Finally, how do women and girls maintain, resist, or otherwise respond as excluded subjects and agents to the rhetoric of masculine becoming that many male youth organizations offer? In what ways are women and girls invested in narratives of masculine becoming? And how do they perform as agents within a Burkean scene? For example, although women are not technically excluded from the appeals of the "Army of One" campaign, they appear to be on the periphery as an audience. In what way did "Army of One" construct identities for potential female recruits? Judith Halberstam's work on female masculinity may provide a starting point for considering how women might identify with rhetorical appeals to a rhetoric of becoming a man.

On the question of what role the organizations in this study play today, I offer a brief example in 2012 Republican presidential primary candidate Rick Perry's 2008 book, *On My Honor: Why the American Values of the Boy Scouts Are Worth Fighting For.* Here Perry situates the BSA, an organization of which he ascended the ranks as a youth, within a grand history of the United States and of Western civilization. While Perry published this book before his 2012 bid for the Republican candidacy, he referred to it and reinterpreted it for audiences of his blog during his campaign. In the book and in Perry's blog posts, he connects the Boy Scouts to his developing identity as an American man and in so doing brings into readers' consciousness the importance of males' proper development.

In Chapter 1 of *On My Honor*, "The Road from Paint Creek," Perry recounts his coming of age as he left his small hometown in Texas:

> Growing up in Paint Creek I thought the things we were taught as Scouts—to do our best to be trustworthy, loyal, helpful, friendly, courteous, kind, obedient, cheerful, thrifty, brave, clean, and reverent—were pretty much what the Founding Fathers had intended for succeeding generations when they created our nation.

The values Perry says he learned as a youth are taken from the text of the Boy Scout Law and become topics he addresses in a later chapter. He juxtaposes his idyllic upbringing that included these values with the cynicism he encountered when he went to college. Describing Texas A&M as a conservative, insulated campus free from dissent, he writes that he heard about counterculture protests elsewhere and implies that this information helped him learn that not every American acts according to Scout values.

In enumerating the elements of the Scout Law, Perry addresses the contemporary cultural implications for the BSA teachings. He suggests that he supports a "don't ask/don't tell" approach to the sexuality of Scouts and Scout Leaders. However, he draws the line at gay Scout Leaders making their orientation public, writing that when a "gay or lesbian leader makes an issue of his or [sic] sexual preference, it makes it impossible to remove sexual conduct from the Scouting realm." He infamously likens homosexuality to alcoholism as a condition that may have a genetic basis but that the afflicted choose to indulge in or to abstain from (Benjamin). Moreover, critics have noted that Perry donated the profits from the sale of his book to the BSA's legal defense fund (Elliott). Ultimately, Perry stands against gay men or women participating in the BSA, but he positions his book as an act of standing *for* long-standing American values in a scene in which those values are threatened. He characterizes the real enemy in the book's American scene as the ACLU, a "minority" that is spreading the "virus of secularism," according to his explanation on his campaign website, "Americans for Rick Perry."

In unreflectively drawing on American commonplaces about the Boy Scouts of America to make his arguments, Perry helps to constitute the rhetoric of becoming masculine for a twenty-first-century American audience. Whether his goal was to make an argument about the culture wars using the BSA as a base, or to make an argument about the BSA using the culture wars as a base, Perry ultimately draws from narratives of boyhood development—both his own narrative and that of the BSA—to make his points. This framing is clearly condensed in his article about his book on his campaign website. There he succinctly frames the scene as a culture war that "the secularists" (whom he alternately refers to as "people on the left") are waging against "people of faith." The war is against institutions that teach the values that young men need in order to enact "a higher calling of living for causes greater than self."

Perry's book associates the BSA with American conservatism. Some of the values he describes—and indeed the values of the Boy Scouts as well as the army's Soldier's Creed and the values described in the Sigma Chi handbook—are values with which people along the political spectrum might agree. But his book is an example of how the ideals of the BSA have formed Perry's identity and how he interprets the process of becoming a man through the rhetorical appeals of the BSA. Michael McGee offers the term *rhetorical idealism* to describe what rhetoricians find in rhetorical documents that constitute identity, like the BSA handbook. He argues that we encounter "material forces, events, and themes in history *only as they have already been mediated or filtered by the Leader whose words [a scholar] studies*" (emphasis in original). The sites in this book provide an example of how this mediation works by constituting an identity as a man-in-the-making, a fundamental character in the story of the American nation.

I am not suggesting that an alternative means of identification would be free of the constitutive effects of rhetoric. The point of this study is not simply to make an assessment of whether male youth organizations are worthy of our participation because they do or do not use appeals to identity using constitutive rhetoric; rather, my aim is to examine how they construct their members.

Americans are surrounded by rhetoric that constitutes males as subjects, and our ideas about how young males become men are as important as our ideas about manhood. At stake in this rhetorical awareness is whether our ideas about male development persist unexamined. Taken individually, many of the values of the male youth organizations discussed in this study could be positive. But produced as holistic narratives that constitute males as true American men in relationship to outsiders, they shape the way we imagine the sexuality, gender, race, and class of American subjects. I hope to have helped to deepen our understanding of this effect of constitutive rhetoric.

NOTES

1. Coming of Age as a Boy in America: Emerging Masculinity as Rhetoric

1. In a classical Marxist context, *ideology* connotes an effect and a force that obscures reality for individuals, rather than a process in which they participate. Many cultural critics, including Raymond Williams, Terry Eagleton, Teun van Dijk, and Stewart Hall, have taken issue with this definition because it neglects the agentive role of audiences in their epistemic process of building identity, and I agree with these critics. However, I would also argue that the agency of boys in this process is often of a different degree from that of older men.

2. I use the term *capitalism* here and elsewhere in this chapter for the sake of making my argument. In using this term, I also acknowledge the complex range of phenomena that intersect to influence national identity, including the struggles between labor and owners of the means of production, the accumulation of wealth for its own sake, the exploitation of the worker, profit through imperialism, and political economy, to name a few.

3. For a useful analysis of the concurrent development of middle-class black masculinity, see Martin Summers.

2. The Rhetorical Performance of Masculine Transformation in the Boy Scouts of America in the Early Twentieth Century

1. See, for example, "The Story of the Unknown Scout" on Scoutingaround.com and "Unknown Scout" on Wikipedia.org. A Google search for "unknown scout" will also turn up several sites maintained by individual BSA troops that recount this story. The official BSA website, www.scouting.org, includes the story on its "Founders" page.

2. See my discussion of neurasthenia in Chapter 1.

3. For example, see Steven Jay Gould's discussion of biological arguments about race in *The Mismeasure of Man* (New York: Norton, 1996).

4. These principles were health, vocational training, social cooperation, worthy use of leisure, worthy home membership, ethical character, and command of fundamental processes (Murray 215).

3. Constituting American Fraternity Members through the Rhetoric of Becoming

1. "Columbia College" and "Columbia University" are sometimes used interchangeably in historical writing about Columbia University. Columbia College is technically the largest undergraduate college within Columbia University. In this chapter, I refer to undergraduate students and the administration of Columbia University as "Columbia."

2. See, for example, Gibson's discussion of Burke on ritual in the context of James George Frazer's 1890 text, *The Golden Bough: A Study in Magic and Religion,* and its explanation of ritual as an anthropological phenomenon.

3. Constantine was the first Roman emperor to convert to Christianity. The evening before the Battle of the Milvian Bridge against Roman Emperor Maxentius in 312 CE, Constantine claimed to have had a vision that led to his conversion to Christianity. According to accounts by historians, in Constantine's vision the Christian God promised victory if Constantine's soldiers painted the sign of the cross on their shields. His army was victorious the next day.

4. The Male Makeover and Emergent Masculine Identity in the "Army of One" Recruitment Campaign

1. I infer that the politically active youth to whom the authors refer are the proportion of the eighteen- to twenty-year-olds who vote in presidential and congressional elections, though the report does not explicitly define this group. Also, the authors' perception that they are interested in "global" issues rather than "national" issues does not appear to be explicitly supported in this report by data or other research.

2. As of 2004, Latino/as constituted 16 percent of the seventeen- to twenty-one-year-old US population (Lovato 16).

3. Between 2000 and 2004, African American recruits fell from 23.5 percent to less than 14.0 percent, "thanks to the widespread disaf-

fection with the Iraq War—and good organizing—among parents and students in the black community" (Lovato 16).

4. In 2003 the total number of US casualties in the wars in Afghanistan and Iraq to that point was 534; in 2004 it was 1,435; and in 2005 it was 2,380, according to the count at icasualties.org.

WORKS CITED

Althusser, Louis. "Ideology and Ideological State Apparatuses: Notes toward an Investigation." *Lenin and Philosophy and Other Essays.* Trans. Ben Brewster. New York: Monthly Review, 1971. 127–86. Print.

Anderson, Benedict. *Imagined Communities: Reflections on the Origin and Spread of Nationalism.* Rev. ed. London: Verso, 2006. Print.

Aristotle. *On Rhetoric: A Theory of Civic Discourse.* Trans. George A. Kennedy. New York: Oxford UP, 1991. Print.

Army of One. Dir. Vic Armstrong. Perf. Dolph Lundgren, George Segal, and Kristian Alfonso. Artisan Entertainment, 1999. DVD. [Original 1993 film title, *Joshua Tree*]

Baden-Powell, Robert. *Aids to Scouting for N.C.O.s and Men.* London: Gale & Polden, 1915. Print.

———. *Rovering to Success: A Guide for Young Manhood.* London: Jenkins, 1964. Print.

———. *Scouting for Boys: A Handbook for Instruction in Good Citizenship.* London: C. Arthur Pearson, 1908. Print.

Balibar, Etienne. "The Nation Form: History and Ideology." *Race, Nation, Class: Ambiguous Identities.* By Etienne Balibar and Immanuel Wallerstein. London: Verso, 1991. 86–106. Print.

Barthes, Roland. "Rhetoric of the Image." *Image, Music, Text.* Comp. and trans. Stephen Heath. New York: Hill, 1977. 32–51. Print.

Beard, George Miller. *American Nervousness, Its Causes and Consequences: A Supplement to Nervous Exhaustion (Neurasthenia).* 1881. Ithaca: Cornell U Library, 2009. Print.

Bederman, Gail. *Manliness and Civilization: A Cultural History of Gender and Race in the United States, 1880–1917.* Chicago: U of Chicago P, 1995. Print.

Begenau, Don. Letter to Editor. *The Ash Can* [Sigma Chi] 6.3 (1954): 2. Box 246, Folder 15. University Archives, Rare Book and Manuscript Library, Columbia University in the City of New York. Print. 9 Jan. 2012.

Beisecker, Barbara. "Rethinking the Rhetorical Situation from within the Thematic of *Différance.*" *Philosophy and Rhetoric* 22 (1989): 110–30. Print.

Benjamin, Mark. "Perry Compared Homosexuality to Alcoholism in 2008 Book." *Time* 24 Aug. 2011. Web.

Bhabha, Homi. *The Location of Culture.* London: Routledge, 1994. Print.

Bhanoo, Sindya N. "A Magnet for Women? Try a Deep Male Voice." *New York Times.* New York Times, 19 Sept. 2011. Web. 5 Dec. 2011.

Billig, Michael. *Banal Nationalism.* London: Sage, 1995. Print.

Bitzer, Lloyd F. "The Rhetorical Situation." *Philosophy and Rhetoric* 1.1 (1968): 1–14. *JSTOR.* Web. 26 Dec. 2011.

Bizzell, Patricia, and Bruce Herzberg. *The Rhetorical Tradition: Readings from Classical Times to the Present.* 2nd ed. Boston: Bedford/St. Martins, 2000. Print.

Boy Scouts of America. *Bear: Cub Scout Book.* Irving: Boy Scouts of America, 1998. Print.

Burke, Kenneth. *Attitudes toward History,* 3rd ed. Berkeley: U of California P, 1984. Print.

———. *A Grammar of Motives.* Berkeley: U of California P, 1969. Print.

———. *Language as Symbolic Action: Essays on Life, Literature, and Method.* Berkeley: U of California P, 1966. Print.

———. *A Rhetoric of Motives.* Berkeley: U of California P, 1969. Print.

Burlas, Joe. "Army Chief of Staff Stress Warrior Ethos for all Soldiers." *Army News Service.* 4 Mar. 2004. Web. 5 July 2006.

Butler, Judith. *Gender Trouble: Feminism and the Subversion of Identity.* New York: Routledge, 1990. Print.

Carnegie, Andrew. "Mr. Carnegie's Word to Boys about War." *Boys' Life: The Boy Scouts' Magazine* 4.9 (1914): 2. National Scouting Museum Archives, Irving, Texas. PDF file. 5 Feb. 2010.

Catano, James V. *Ragged Dicks: Masculinity, Steel, and the Rhetoric of the Self-Made Man.* Carbondale: Southern Illinois UP, 2001. Print.

Charland, Maurice. "Constitutive Rhetoric: The Case of the *Peuple Québécois.*" *Quarterly Journal of Speech* 73.2 (1987): 133–50. Print.

Church, Michael J., ed. *The Norman Shield: Reference Manual of the Sigma Chi Fraternity.* 43rd ed. N.p.: Sigma Chi Fraternity, 2009. Print.

Clark, Gregory. *Rhetorical Landscapes in America: Variations on a Theme from Kenneth Burke.* Columbia: U of South Carolina P, 2004. Print.

Connell, R. W. *Masculinities,* 2nd ed. Berkeley, U of California P, 2005. Print.

Conners, Robert J. "Teaching and Learning as a Man." *College English* 58.2 (1996): 137–57. Print.

Dao, James. "Ad Now Seeks Recruits for 'An Army of One.'" *New York Times*. New York Times, 10 Jan. 2001. Web. 14 March 2011.

Duara, Prasenjit. "Historicizing National Identity, or Who Imagines What and When." *Eley and Suny* 151–177.

Dunn, Bill. "Ceremonies Section from the 1995 Suffolk County Pow Wow Book." 25 Feb. 1996. Web. 28 Nov. 2001. <http://www.wtrfrd.com/pack339/339cere.htm>.

Eley, Geoff, and Ronald Grigor Suny, eds. *Becoming National: A Reader.* New York: Oxford UP, 1996. Print.

Elliott, Justin. "What I Learned about Rick Perry from Reading His Bizarre Book about the Boy Scouts." *New Republic* 15 Sept. 2011. Web. 16 Feb. 2016.

Enloe, Cynthia. *Bananas, Beaches, and Bases: Making Feminist Sense of International Politics.* Berkeley: U of California P, 1990. Print.

Evans, Brad, and Henry A. Giroux. *Disposable Futures: The Seduction of Violence in the Age of Spectacle.* San Francisco: City Lights, 2015. Print.

Farrell, Thomas B. "Rhetoric in History as Theory and Praxis: A Blast from the Past." *Philosophy and Rhetoric* 41.4 (2008): 323–36. *Project Muse.* Web. 8 Jan 2010.

Foss, Sonja K. "Ambiguity as Persuasion: The Vietnam Veterans Memorial." *Communication Quarterly* 34.3 (1986): 326–40. Web. 23 Sept. 2015.

———. "A Rhetorical Schema for the Evaluation of Visual Imagery." *Communication Studies* 45.3–4 (1994): 213–24. *ProQuest.* Web. 10 Aug. 2015.

"Fraternities at Columbia." *Columbia College Today* Spring 1962: 13–17. Series XIX.3, Box 246, Folder 21. University Archives, Rare Book and Manuscript Library, Columbia University in the City of New York. Print. 9 Jan. 2012.

"Fraternities' Future in Doubt." *The Columbia Daily Spectator* 19 Sept. 1967. Series XIX.3, Box 246, Folder 21. University Archives, Rare Book and Manuscript Library, Columbia University in the City of New York. Print. 9 Jan. 2012.

Freud, Sigmund. "My Views on the Part Played by Sexuality in the Etiology of the Neuroses." *The Standard Edition of the Complete Psychological Works of Sigmund Freud.* Trans. James Strachey. Vol. 7. London: Hogarth, 1953. 269–79. Print.

Fuss, Diana. *Identification Papers.* New York: Routledge, 1995. Print.

Gellner, Ernest. *Nations and Nationalism.* Ithaca: Cornell UP, 1983. Print.

Gibson, Keith. "Burke, Frazer, and Ritual: Attitudes toward Attitudes." *KB Journal* 3.1 (2006). Web. 10 July 2013.

Gillette, Joshua C. "SFARFS Members Regroup to Organize Strategy for Future." *Columbia Daily Spectator* 16 Sept. 1988. Series XIX.3, Box 246, Folder 21. University Archives, Rare Book and Manuscript Library, Columbia University in the City of New York. Print. 9 Jan. 2012.

Giroux, Henry A. *America on the Edge: Henry Giroux on Politics, Culture, and Education*. New York: Palgrave-MacMillan, 2006. Print.

Grabenstein, Daniel E. "President's State of the Fraternity Address." *The Ash Can* [Sigma Chi] 6.3 (1954): 3. Box 246, Folder 15. University Archives, Rare Book and Manuscript Library, Columbia University in the City of New York. Print. 9 Jan. 2012.

Greene, Ronald Walter. "The Aesthetic Turn and the Rhetorical Perspective on Argumentation." *Argumentation and Advocacy* 35.1 (1998). *ProQuest*. Web. 10 Aug. 2015.

Gura, Sheryl Anne. "Fraternities: A Decade of Change." *The Columbia Daily Spectator* 29 Oct. 1971. Series XIX.3, Box 246, Folder 21. University Archives, Rare Book and Manuscript Library, Columbia University in the City of New York. Print. 9 Jan. 2012.

Haberman, Clyde. "NYC; Army of One Is Missing Sense of Duty." *New York Times*. New York Times, 20 Jan. 2001. Web. 14 March 2011.

Halberstam, Judith. *Female Masculinity*. Durham: Duke UP, 1998. Print.

Hall, G. Stanley. *Adolescence: Its Psychology and Its Relations to Physiology, Anthropology, Sociology, Sex, Crime, Religion and Education*. 1904. Nabu, 2006. Kindle file.

Hall, Kevin. "The Boys Build Again: Restoration of Columbia's Fraternities." *Sundial Alumni Newsletter* 5 May 1983: 4. Series XIX.3, Box 246, Folder 21. University Archives, Rare Book and Manuscript Library, Columbia University in the City of New York. Print. 9 Jan. 2012.

Hantover, Jeffrey P. "The Boy Scouts and the Validation of Masculinity." *Journal of Social Issues* 34.1 (1978): 184–95. Web. 4 Aug. 2010.

Harris, Cheryl. "Whiteness as Property." *Harvard Law Review* 106.8 (1993): 1707–1791. *JSTOR*. Web. 10 June 2013.

Helmers, Marguerite. "Framing the Fine Arts through Rhetoric." Hill and Helmers 63–86.

Hill, Charles A., and Marguerite Helmers, eds. *Defining Visual Rhetorics*. London: Erlbaum, 2004. Print.

Hunt, John. "All Around the Circle." *Scouting* 7.18 (1919): 4. Web. 24 Mar. 2016.

Hunter, Ian. *Rethinking the School: Subjectivity, Bureaucracy, Criticism*. New York: St. Martin's Press, 1994. Print.

Jasinski, James. "Constitutive Rhetoric." *Sourcebook on Rhetoric: Key Concepts in Contemporary Rhetorical Studies*. London: Sage, 2001. 106–08. *Google Book Search*. Web. 11 Jan. 2011.

Kaplan, Amy. *The Anarchy of Empire in the Making of U.S. Culture*. Cambridge: Harvard UP, 2002. Print.

Kaufman, David. "Greek System Still on Rise Despite Recent Opposition." *Columbia Daily Spectator* 17 Sept. 1988. Series XIX.3, Box 246, Folder 21. University Archives, Rare Book and Manuscript Library, Columbia University in the City of New York. Print. 9 Jan. 2012.

Kelso, Stephen. "Fraternities Are a Necessity!" *Columbia College Today* Spring 1962:18. Series XIX.3, Box 246, Folder 21. University Archives, Rare Book and Manuscript Library, Columbia University in the City of New York. Print. 9 Jan. 2012.

Kimbrell, Curtis L. Non-Commissioned Officer of the Year Presentation. 2004. U.S. Army Space and Missile Defense Command/U.S. Army Strategic Forces Command. Web. 5 July 2006.

Kipling, Rudyard. *The Jungle Book*. London: MacMillan, 1894. Print.

Kress, Gunther, and Theo van Leeuwen. *Reading Images: The Grammar of Visual Design*. 2nd ed. London: Routledge, 2006. Print.

LaMotte, CPT Joshua J. "The Warrior Ethos and Basic Combat Training." *Quartermaster Professional Bulletin* Spring (2004). Web. 15 Feb. 2016.

Lee, Jean. "FOCUS: Should the Frats Be Forced to Go Co-ed?" *Columbia Daily Spectator* 30 Oct. 1989. Series XIX.3, Box 246, Folder 21. University Archives, Rare Book and Manuscript Library, Columbia University in the City of New York. Print. 9 Jan. 2012.

Loewe, Drew. "Where Human Relations Grandly Converge: The Constitutional Dialectic of Hizb ut-Tahrir." *KB Journal* 7.2 (2011). Web. 23 Sept. 2015.

Lovato, Roberto. "The War for Latinos." *The Nation* 3 Oct. 2005: 14–18. Print.

Lowe, Lisa. *Immigrant Acts: On Asian American Cultural Politics*. Durham: Duke UP, 1996. Print.

MacDonald, Robert H. *Sons of the Empire: The Frontier and the Boy Scout Movement, 1890–1918*. Toronto: U of Toronto P, 1993. Print.

McGee, Michael Calvin. "In Search of the 'The People': A Rhetorical Alternative." *Quarterly Journal of Speech* 61.3 (1975): 235–49. *Communication and Mass Media Complete*. 28 Mar. 2011.

McManus, Lindsay Green. *Performing Masculinity: Control, Manhood, and the Rhetoric of Effeminacy*. Diss. U of South Carolina, 2007. Ann Arbor: UMI. *Google Book Search*. Web. 23 Sept. 2015.

Meier, Peter. "Coed Fraternity Proposal Prompts Shouting Match." *Columbia Daily Spectator* 29 Feb. 1988. Series XIX.3, Box 246, Folder 21. University Archives, Rare Book and Manuscript Library, Columbia University in the City of New York. Print. 9 Jan. 2012.

———. "Frat Forum Will Provide Focus for Campus Debate." *Columbia Daily Spectator* 12 April 1988. Series XIX.3, Box 246, Folder 21. University Archives, Rare Book and Manuscript Library, Columbia University in the City of New York. Print. 9 Jan. 2012.

Meier, Peter, and Schultz, Evan. "SFARFS Claims Beer Bath Courtesy of Frat." *Columbia Daily Spectator* 21 Nov. 1988. Series XIX.3, Box 246, Folder 21. University Archives, Rare Book and Manuscript Library, Columbia University in the City of New York. Print. 9 Jan. 2012.

Minov, Norm. Report. *The Ash Can* [Sigma Chi] 9.1 (1956): 5. Box 246, Folder 15. University Archives, Rare Book and Manuscript Library, Columbia University in the City of New York. Print. 9 Jan. 2012.

Moran, Carlos. "Latinos Need Strong Education, Not Army." *Daily Sundial* 22 Nov. 2005. Web. 18 June 2006.

Moskos, Charles. "Reviving the Citizen Soldier." *Public Interest* 147 (2002): 76–86. Print.

Mountford, Roxanne. *The Gendered Pulpit: Preaching in American Protestant Spaces.* Carbondale: Southern Illinois UP, 2003. Print.

Murray, William D. *The History of the Boy Scouts of America.* New York: Boy Scouts of America, 1937. Print.

National Research Council. *Attitudes, Aptitudes, and Aspirations of American Youth: Implications for Military Recruitment.* Washington: National Academies, 2003. Print.

Nelson, Dana D. *National Manhood: Capitalist Citizenship and the Imagined Fraternity of White Men.* Durham: Duke UP, 1998. Print.

"Non-Bias Oath at Sigma Chi Looks Dubious." *Columbia Daily Spectator* 2 Oct. 1964. Sigma Chi (Scientific Honor Fraternity) 1880s–1980, Box 248, Folder 8. University Archives, Rare Book and Manuscript Library, Columbia University in the City of New York. Print. 9 Jan. 2012.

Olson, Christa. "Burke's Attitude Problem." *College Composition and Communication* 60.2 (2008): W19–29. Web. 24 April 2012.

Oyos, Matthew M. "Theodore Roosevelt and the Implements of War." *Journal of Military History* 60.4 (1996): 631–55. *JSTOR.* Web. 12 Feb. 2016.

———. "Theodore Roosevelt, Congress, and the Military: U.S. Civil-Military Relations in the Early Twentieth Century." *Presidential Studies Quarterly* 30.2 (2000): 312–30. *InfoTrac.* Web. 28 June 2005.

Perry, Rick. "'On My Honor': Why I Wrote This Book." *Americans for Rick Perry*. 20 Feb. 2008. Web. 14 July 2011.

Perry, Rick. *On My Honor: Why the American Values of the Boy Scouts Are Worth Fighting For*. Macon: Stroud & Hall, 2008. Kindle file.

Peterson, Robert W. *The Boy Scouts: An American Adventure*. Winter Park: Houghton, 1984. Print.

Petterchak, Janice A. *Lone Scout: W. D. Boyce and American Boy Scouting*. Rochester: Legacy, 2003. Print.

Ratcliffe, Krista. *Rhetorical Listening: Identification, Gender, Whiteness*. Carbondale: Southern Illinois UP, 2006. Print.

Renan, Ernest. "What Is a Nation?" Eley and Suny 42–55.

Rickert, Thomas. *Acts of Enjoyment: Rhetoric, Zizek, and the Return of the Subject*. Pittsburgh: U of Pittsburgh P, 2007. Kindle file.

Roosevelt, Theodore. "The Expansion of the White Races." [Address at the Celebration of the African Diamond Jubilee of the Methodist Episcopal Church, Washington, D.C., January 18, 1909]. *Two Essays by Theodore Roosevelt*. Ed. Cary Nelson. *Modern American Poetry*. Web. 16 July 2005. <http://www.english.uiuc.edu/Maps/poets/a_f/espada/roosevelt.htm>.

Rotundo, E. Anthony. *American Manhood: Transformations in Masculinity from the Revolution to the Modern Era*. New York: Basic, 1993. Print.

Rowan, Edward L. *To Do My Best: James E. West and the History of the Boy Scouts of America*. Las Vegas: Las Vegas International Scouting Museum, 2005. Print.

Shanker, Thom. "Army and Other Ground Forces Meet '06 Recruiting Goals." *New York Times* 10 Oct. 2006: A19. Print.

Smith, Anthony D. "Gastronomy or Geology? The Role of Nationalism in the Reconstruction of Nations." *Nations and Nationalism* 1.1 (1995): 3–23. Print.

———. "The Origins of Nations." Eley and Suny 106–130.

Stein, Sarah R. "The '1984' Macintosh Ad: Cinematic Icons and Constitutive Rhetoric in the Launch of a New Machine." *Quarterly Journal of Speech* 88.2 (2002): 169–92. Print.

"The Story of the Unknown Scout." *ScoutingAround.com*. Scoutingaround.com, 2008. Web. 4 Aug. 2010.

Summers, Martin. *Manliness and Its Discontents: The Black Middle Class and the Transformation of Masculinity, 1900–1930*. Chapel Hill: U of North Carolina P, 2004. Print.

Swartz, Omar. *The Rise of Rhetoric and Its Intersections with Contemporary Critical Thought*. Boulder: Westview, 1998. Print.

Syrett, Nicholas L. *The Company He Keeps: A History of White College Fraternities.* Chapel Hill: U of North Carolina P, 2009. Print.

Tate, Helen. "The Ideological Effects of a Failed Constitutive Rhetoric: The Co-option of the Rhetoric of White Lesbian Feminism." *Women's Studies in Communication* 28:1 (2005): 1–31. *Academic Search Complete.* Web. 5 Jan. 2011.

Trebay, Guy. "From Boys to Men." *New York Times.* New York Times, 15 Oct. 2010. Web. 5 Dec. 2011.

United States. Dept. of the Army. "The Soldier's Creed." *The Soldier's Guide.* [Dept. of the Army Field Manual FM 21-13]. Washington: Dept. of the Army, 1961. 125–26. Print.

"Unknown Scout." *Wikipedia: The Free Encyclopedia.* Wikipedia, 6 June 2010. Web. 4 Aug. 2010.

Vatz, Richard E. "The Myth of the Rhetorical Situation." *Philosophy and Rhetoric* 6.3 (1973): 154–61. Print.

Winslow, Luke A. "Style and Struggle: The Rhetoric of Masculinity." Diss. U of Texas at Austin, 2009. *U of Texas Libraries.* Web. 23 Sept. 2015.

INDEX

AUTHOR

Leigh Ann Jones is an assistant professor of English at Hunter College of the City University of New York, where she teaches rhetorical criticism and history, composition, and pedagogy in the undergraduate and graduate programs. She also codirects Hunter's first-year writing course. In addition to her work on rhetorics of national masculinity, Jones has published on performative epistemology, a multimodal approach to composition pedagogy.

BOOKS IN THE CCCC STUDIES IN WRITING & RHETORIC SERIES

From Boys to Men: Rhetorics of Emergent American Masculinity
Leigh Ann Jones

Freedom Writing: African American Civil Rights Literacy Activism, 1955–1967
Rhea Estelle Lathan

The Desire for Literacy: Writing in the Lives of Adult Learners
Lauren Rosenberg

On Multimodality: New Media in Composition Studies
Jonathan Alexander and Jacqueline Rhodes

Toward a New Rhetoric of Difference
Stephanie L. Kerschbaum

Rhetoric of Respect: Recognizing Change at a Community Writing Center
Tiffany Rousculp

After Pedagogy: The Experience of Teaching
Paul Lynch

Redesigning Composition for Multilingual Realities
Jay Jordan

Agency in the Age of Peer Production
Quentin D. Vieregge, Kyle D. Stedman, Taylor Joy Mitchell, and Joseph M. Moxley

Remixing Composition: A History of Multimodal Writing Pedagogy
Jason Palmeri

First Semester: Graduate Students, Teaching Writing, and the Challenge of Middle Ground
Jessica Restaino

Agents of Integration: Understanding Transfer as a Rhetorical Act
Rebecca S. Nowacek

Digital Griots: African American Rhetoric in a Multimedia Age
Adam J. Banks

The Managerial Unconscious in the History of Composition Studies
Donna Strickland

Everyday Genres: Writing Assignments across the Disciplines
Mary Soliday

The Community College Writer: Exceeding Expectations
Howard Tinberg and Jean-Paul Nadeau

A Taste for Language: Literacy, Class, and English Studies
James Ray Watkins

Before Shaughnessy: Basic Writing at Yale and Harvard, 1920–1960
Kelly Ritter

Writer's Block: The Cognitive Dimension
Mike Rose

Teaching/Writing in Thirdspaces: The Studio Approach
Rhonda C. Grego and Nancy S. Thompson

Rural Literacies
Kim Donehower, Charlotte Hogg, and Eileen E. Schell

Writing with Authority: Students' Roles as Writers in Cross-National Perspective
David Foster

Whistlin' and Crowin' Women of Appalachia: Literacy Practices since College
Katherine Kelleher Sohn

Sexuality and the Politics of Ethos in the Writing Classroom
Zan Meyer Gonçalves

This book was typeset in Garamond and Frutiger by Barbara Frazier.
Typefaces used on the cover include Adobe Garamond and Formata.
The book was printed on 55-lb. Natural Offset paper
by King Printing Company, Inc.

www.ingramcontent.com/pod-product-compliance
Lightning Source LLC
Chambersburg PA
CBHW070732270326
41926CB00054B/3088